Beowulf

Translated by
Burton Raffel

and Related Readings

McDougal Littell
A HOUGHTON MIFFLIN COMPANY
Evanston, Illinois • Boston • Dallas

Acknowledgments

Dutton Signet: *Beowulf* by Burton Raffel, translator, translated by Burton Raffel. Translation copyright © 1963 by Burton Raffel. Afterword copyright © 1963 by New American Library. Used by permission of Dutton Signet, a division of Penguin Books USA Inc.

Yale University Press: "The Wanderer," from *Poems and Prose from the Old English,* translated by Burton Raffel, edited by Burton Raffel and Alexandra Olsen. Reprinted by permission of Yale University Press.

Harcourt Brace & Company: "Beowulf," from *Ceremony and Other Poems* by Richard Wilbur. Copyright 1950 and renewed 1978 by Richard Wilbur. Reprinted by permission of Harcourt Brace & Company.

Alfred A. Knopf, Inc.: Excerpt from *Grendel* by John Gardner. Copyright © 1971 by John Gardner. Reprinted by permission of Alfred A. Knopf, Inc.

Workman Publishing Company, Inc.: "Beowulf," from *Shrinklits* by Maurice Sagoff. Copyright © 1970, 1980 by Maurice Sagoff. Used by permission of Workman Publishing Company, Inc.

Houghton Mifflin Company: Excerpts from *Gilgamesh* by Herbert Mason. Copyright © 1970 by Herbert Mason. Reprinted by permission of Houghton Mifflin Company. All rights reserved.

Continued on page 190

Cover illustration by Liz Pyle.

Printed in the United States of America.

ISBN 0-395-90109-X

3 4 5 6 7 8 9 QNT 03 02 01 00

Contents

Beowulf

Translated by

Burton Raffel

Prologue

Hear me! We've heard of Danish heroes,
Ancient kings and the glory they cut
For themselves, swinging mighty swords!
   How Shild* made slaves of soldiers from
     every
5   Land, crowds of captives he'd beaten
Into terror; he'd traveled to Denmark alone,
An abandoned child, but changed his own
     fate,
Lived to be rich and much honored. He ruled
Lands on all sides: wherever the sea
10 Would take them his soldiers sailed, returned
With tribute and obedience. There was a
     brave
King! And he gave them more than his glory,
Conceived a son for the Danes, a new leader
Allowed them by the grace of God. They had
     lived,
15 Before his coming, kingless and miserable;
Now the Lord of all life, Ruler
Of glory, blessed them with a prince, Beo,*
Whose power and fame soon spread through
     the world.
Shild's strong son was the glory of Denmark;
20 His father's warriors were wound round his
     heart
With golden rings, bound to their prince
By his father's treasure. So young men build

---

* This mark indicates that the word appears in the Glossary.

The future, wisely open-handed in peace,
Protected in war; so warriors earn
25 Their fame, and wealth is shaped with a
sword.
When his time was come the old king died,
Still strong but called to the Lord's hands.
His comrades carried him down to the shore,
Bore him as their leader had asked, their lord
30 And companion, while words could move on
his tongue.
Shild's reign had been long; he'd ruled them
well.
There in the harbor was a ring-prowed
fighting
Ship, its timbers icy, waiting,
And there they brought the belovèd body
35 Of their ring-giving lord, and laid him near
The mast. Next to that noble corpse
They heaped up treasures, jeweled helmets,
Hooked swords and coats of mail, armor
Carried from the ends of the earth: no ship
40 Had ever sailed so brightly fitted,
No king sent forth more deeply mourned.
Forced to set him adrift, floating
As far as the tide might run, they refused
To give him less from their hoards of gold
45 Than those who'd shipped him away, an
orphan
And a beggar, to cross the waves alone.
High up over his head they flew
His shining banner, then sadly let
The water pull at the ship, watched it
50 Slowly sliding to where neither rulers
Nor heroes nor anyone can say whose hands
Opened to take that motionless cargo.

1

Then Beo was king in that Danish castle,
Shild's son ruling as long as his father
55 And as loved, a famous lord of men.
And he in turn gave his people a son,
The great Healfdane,* a fierce fighter
Who led the Danes to the end of his long
Life and left them four children,
60 Three princes to guide them in battle, Hergar*
And Hrothgar* and Halga* the Good, and
    one daughter,
Yrs,* who was given to Onela,* king
Of the Swedes, and became his wife and their
    queen.
Then Hrothgar, taking the throne, led
65 The Danes to such glory that comrades and
    kinsmen
Swore by his sword, and young men swelled
His armies, and he thought of greatness and
    resolved
To build a hall that would hold his mighty
Band and reach higher toward Heaven than
    anything
70 That had ever been known to the sons of
    men.
And in that hall he'd divide the spoils
Of their victories, to old and young what
    they'd earned
In battle, but leaving the common pastures
Untouched, and taking no lives. The work
75 Was ordered, the timbers tied and shaped
By the hosts that Hrothgar ruled. It was
    quickly
Ready, that most beautiful of dwellings, built

As he'd wanted, and then he whose word was
         obeyed
All over the earth named it Herot.*
80 His boast come true he commanded a
         banquet,
Opened out his treasure-full hands.
That towering place, gabled and huge,
Stood waiting for time to pass, for war
To begin, for flames to leap as high
85 As the feud that would light them, and for
         Herot to burn.
      A powerful monster, living down
In the darkness, growled in pain, impatient
As day after day the music rang
Loud in that hall, the harp's rejoicing
90 Call and the poet's clear songs, sung
Of the ancient beginnings of us all, recalling
The Almighty making the earth, shaping
These beautiful plains marked off by oceans,
Then proudly setting the sun and moon
95 To glow across the land and light it;
The corners of the earth were made lovely
         with trees
And leaves, made quick with life, with each
Of the nations who now move on its face.
         And then
As now warriors sang of their pleasure:
100 So Hrothgar's men lived happy in his hall
Till the monster stirred, that demon, that
         fiend,
Grendel,* who haunted the moors, the wild
Marshes, and made his home in a hell
Not hell but earth. He was spawned in that
         slime,
105 Conceived by a pair of those monsters born
Of Cain, murderous creatures banished

By God, punished forever for the crime
Of Abel's death. The Almighty drove
Those demons out, and their exile was bitter,
110 Shut away from men; they split
Into a thousand forms of evil—spirits
And fiends, goblins, monsters, giants,
A brood forever opposing the Lord's
Will, and again and again defeated.

2

115   Then, when darkness had dropped, Grendel
Went up to Herot, wondering what the
     warriors
Would do in that hall when their drinking
     was done.
He found them sprawled in sleep, suspecting
Nothing, their dreams undisturbed. The
     monster's
120 Thoughts were as quick as his greed or his
     claws:
He slipped through the door and there in the
     silence
Snatched up thirty men, smashed them
Unknowing in their beds and ran out with
     their bodies,
The blood dripping behind him, back
125 To his lair, delighted with his night's slaughter.
    At daybreak, with the sun's first light, they
     saw
How well he had worked, and in that gray
     morning
Broke their long feast with tears and laments

For the dead. Hrothgar, their lord, sat joyless
130 In Herot, a mighty prince mourning
The fate of his lost friends and companions,
Knowing by its tracks that some demon had
   torn
His followers apart. He wept, fearing
The beginning might not be the end. And that
   night
135 Grendel came again, so set
On murder that no crime could ever be
   enough,
No savage assault quench his lust
For evil. Then each warrior tried
To escape him, searched for rest in different
140 Beds, as far from Herot as they could find,
Seeing how Grendel hunted when they slept.
Distance was safety; the only survivors
Were those who fled him. Hate had
   triumphed.
   So Grendel ruled, fought with the
   righteous,
145 One against many, and won; so Herot
Stood empty, and stayed deserted for years,
Twelve winters of grief for Hrothgar, king
Of the Danes, sorrow heaped at his door
By hell-forged hands. His misery leaped
150 The seas, was told and sung in all
Men's ears: how Grendel's hatred began,
How the monster relished his savage war
On the Danes, keeping the bloody feud
Alive, seeking no peace, offering
155 No truce, accepting no settlement, no price
In gold or land, and paying the living
For one crime only with another. No one
Waited for reparation from his plundering
   claws:

That shadow of death hunted in the darkness,
160 Stalked Hrothgar's warriors, old
And young, lying in waiting, hidden
In mist, invisibly following them from the edge
Of the marsh, always there, unseen.
    So mankind's enemy continued his crimes,
165 Killing as often as he could, coming
Alone, bloodthirsty and horrible. Though he
        lived
In Herot, when the night hid him, he never
Dared to touch king Hrothgar's glorious
Throne, protected by God—God,
170 Whose love Grendel could not know. But
        Hrothgar's
Heart was bent. The best and most noble
Of his council debated remedies, sat
In secret sessions, talking of terror
And wondering what the bravest of warriors
        could do.
175 And sometimes they sacrificed to the old stone
        gods,
Made heathen vows, hoping for Hell's
Support, the Devil's guidance in driving
Their affliction off. That was their way,
And the heathen's only hope, Hell
180 Always in their hearts, knowing neither God
Nor His passing as He walks through our
        world, the Lord
Of Heaven and earth; their ears could not hear
His praise nor know His glory. Let them
Beware, those who are thrust into danger,
185 Clutched at by trouble, yet can carry no solace
In their hearts, cannot hope to be better! Hail
To those who will rise to God, drop off
Their dead bodies and seek our Father's peace!

3

So the living sorrow of Healfdane's son
190 Simmered, bitter and fresh, and no wisdom
Or strength could break it: that agony hung
On king and people alike, harsh
And unending, violent and cruel, and evil.
In his far-off home Beowulf,* Higlac's*
195 Follower and the strongest of the Geats*—
greater
And stronger than anyone anywhere in this
world—
Heard how Grendel filled nights with horror
And quickly commanded a boat fitted out,
Proclaiming that he'd go to that famous king,
200 Would sail across the sea to Hrothgar,
Now when help was needed. None
Of the wise ones regretted his going, much
As he was loved by the Geats: the omens were
good,
And they urged the adventure on. So Beowulf
205 Chose the mightiest men he could find,
The bravest and best of the Geats, fourteen
In all, and led them down to their boat;
He knew the sea, would point the prow
Straight to that distant Danish shore.
210 Then they sailed, set their ship
Out on the waves, under the cliffs.
Ready for what came they wound through the
currents,
The seas beating at the sand, and were borne
In the lap of their shining ship, lined
215 With gleaming armor, going safely
In that oak-hard boat to where their hearts
took them.

The wind hurried them over the waves,
The ship foamed through the sea like a bird
Until, in the time they had known it would
    take,
220 Standing in the round-curled prow they could
    see
Sparkling hills, high and green,
Jutting up over the shore, and rejoicing
In those rock-steep cliffs they quietly ended
Their voyage. Jumping to the ground, the
    Geats
225 Pushed their boat to the sand and tied it
In place, mail shirts and armor rattling
As they swiftly moored their ship. And then
They gave thanks to God for their easy
    crossing.
    High on a wall a Danish watcher
230 Patrolling along the cliffs saw
The travelers crossing to the shore, their
    shields
Raised and shining; he came riding down,
Hrothgar's lieutenant, spurring his horse,
Needing to know why they'd landed, these
    men
235 In armor. Shaking his heavy spear
In their faces he spoke:
                "Whose soldiers are you,
You who've been carried in your deep-keeled
    ship
Across the sea-road to this country of mine?
240 Listen! I've stood on these cliffs longer
Than you know, keeping our coast free
Of pirates, raiders sneaking ashore
From their ships, seeking our lives and our
    gold.
None have ever come more openly—

245 And yet you've offered no password, no sign
From my prince, no permission from my
people for your landing
Here. Nor have I ever seen,
Out of all the men on earth, one greater
Than has come with you; no commoner
carries
250 Such weapons, unless his appearance, and his
beauty,
Are both lies. You! Tell me your name,
And your father's; no spies go further onto
Danish
Soil than you've come already. Strangers,
From wherever it was you sailed, tell it,
255 And tell it quickly, the quicker the better,
I say, for us all. Speak, say
Exactly who you are, and from where, and
why."

4

Their leader answered him, Beowulf
unlocking
Words from deep in his breast:
260   "We are Geats,
Men who follow Higlac. My father
Was a famous soldier, known far and wide
As a leader of men. His name was Edgetho*.
His life lasted many winters;
265 Wise men all over the earth surely
Remember him still. And we have come
seeking
Your prince, Healfdane's son, protector

Of this people, only in friendship: instruct us,
Watchman, help us with your words! Our
    errand
270 Is a great one, our business with the glorious
    king
Of the Danes no secret; there's nothing dark
Or hidden in our coming. You know (if we've
    heard
The truth, and been told honestly) that your
    country
Is cursed with some strange, vicious creature
275 That hunts only at night and that no one
Has seen. It's said, watchman, that he has
    slaughtered
Your people, brought terror to the darkness.
    Perhaps
Hrothgar can hunt, here in my heart,
For some way to drive this devil out—
280 If anything will ever end the evils
Afflicting your wise and famous lord.
Here he can cool his burning sorrow.
Or else he may see his suffering go on
Forever, for as long as Herot towers
285 High on your hills."
                  The mounted officer
Answered him bluntly, the brave watchman:
    "A soldier should know the difference
    between words
And deeds, and keep that knowledge clear
290 In his brain. I believe your words, I trust in
Your friendship. Go forward, weapons and
    armor
And all, on into Denmark. I'll guide you
Myself—and my men will guard your ship,
Keep it safe here on our shores,
295 Your fresh-tarred boat, watch it well,

Until that curving prow carries
Across the sea to Geatland a chosen
Warrior who bravely does battle with the
    creature
Haunting our people, who survives that
    horror
300   Unhurt, and goes home bearing our love."
     Then they moved on. Their boat lay moored,
Tied tight to its anchor. Glittering at the top
Of their golden helmets wild boar heads
    gleamed,
Shining decorations, swinging as they marched,
305   Erect like guards, like sentinels, as though
    ready
To fight. They marched, Beowulf and his men
And their guide, until they could see the gables
Of Herot, covered with hammered gold
And glowing in the sun—that most famous of
    all dwellings,
310   Towering majestic, its glittering roofs
Visible far across the land.
Their guide reined in his horse, pointing
To that hall, built by Hrothgar for the best
And bravest of his men; the path was plain,
315   They could see their way. And then he spoke:
    "Now I must leave you: may the Lord our
    God
Protect your coming and going! The sea
Is my job, keeping these coasts free
Of invaders, bands of pirates: I must go back."

5

320 The path he'd shown them was paved, cobbled
Like a Roman road. They arrived with their
    mail shirts
Glittering, silver-shining links
Clanking an iron song as they came.
Sea-weary still, they set their broad,
325 Battle-hardened shields in rows
Along the wall, then stretched themselves
On Herot's benches. Their armor rang;
Their ash-wood spears stood in a line,
Gray-tipped and straight: the Geats' war-gear
330 Were honored weapons.
                  A Danish warrior
Asked who they were, their names and their
    fathers':
    "Where have you carried these gold-carved
    shields from,
These silvery shirts and helmets, and those
    spears
335 Set out in long lines? I am Hrothgar's
Herald and captain. Strangers have come here
Before, but never so freely, so bold.
And you come too proudly to be exiles: not
    poverty
But your hearts' high courage has brought you
    to Hrothgar."
340   He was answered by a famous soldier, the
    Geats'
Proud prince:
              "We follow Higlac, break bread
At his side. I am Beowulf. My errand
Is for Healfdane's great son to hear, your
    glorious

345 Lord; if he chooses to receive us we will greet
        him,
     Salute the chief of the Danes and speak out
     Our message."
                      Wulfgar* replied—a prince
     Born to the Swedes, famous for both strength
350 And wisdom:
                      "Our warmhearted lord will be
        told
     Of your coming; I shall tell our king, our
        giver
     Of bright rings, and hurry back with his
        word,
     And speak it here, however he answers
355 Your request."
                      He went quickly to where
        Hrothgar sat,
     Gray and old, in the middle of his men,
     And knowing the custom of that court
        walked straight
     To the king's great chair, stood waiting to be
        heard,
360 Then spoke:
                      "There are Geats who have come
        sailing the open
     Ocean to our land, come far over
     The high waves, led by a warrior
     Called Beowulf. They wait on your word,
        bring messages
365 For your ears alone. My lord, grant them
     A gracious answer, see them and hear
     What they've come for! Their weapons and
        armor are nobly
     Worked—these men are no beggars. And
        Beowulf

Their prince, who showed them the way to
   our shores,
370 Is a mighty warrior, powerful and wise."

6

   The Danes' high prince and protector
      answered:
   "I knew Beowulf as a boy. His father
   Was Edgetho, who was given Hrethel's* one
      daughter
   —Hrethel, Higlac's father. Now Edgetho's
375 Brave son is here, come visiting a friendly
   King. And I've heard that when seamen came,
   Bringing their gifts and presents to the Geats,
   They wrestled and ran together, and Higlac's
   Young prince showed them a mighty battle-
      grip,
380 Hands that moved with thirty men's strength,
   And courage to match. Our Holy Father
   Has sent him as a sign of His grace, a mark
   Of His favor, to help us defeat Grendel
   And end that terror. I shall greet him with
      treasures,
385 Gifts to reward his courage in coming to us.
   Quickly, order them all to come to me
   Together, Beowulf and his band of Geats.
   And tell them, too, how welcome we will make
      them!"
   Then Wulfgar went to the door and
      addressed
390 The waiting seafarers with soldier's words:

"My lord, the great king of the Danes,
        commands me
To tell you that he knows of your noble birth
And that having come to him from over the
        open
Sea you have come bravely and are welcome.
395   Now go to him as you are, in your armor and
        helmets,
But leave your battle-shields here, and your
        spears,
Let them lie waiting for the promises your
        words
May make."
                    Beowulf arose, with his men
400   Around him, ordering a few to remain
With their weapons, leading the others quickly
Along under Herot's steep roof into Hrothgar's
Presence. Standing on that prince's own hearth,
Helmeted, the silvery metal of his mail shirt
405   Gleaming with a smith's high art, he greeted
The Danes' great lord:
                    "Hail, Hrothgar!
Higlac is my cousin and my king; the days
Of my youth have been filled with glory. Now
        Grendel's
410   Name has echoed in our land: sailors
Have brought us stories of Herot, the best
Of all mead-halls, deserted and useless when
        the moon
Hangs in skies the sun had lit,
Light and life fleeing together.
415   My people have said, the wisest, most knowing
And best of them, that my duty was to go to
        the Danes'
Great king. They have seen my strength for
        themselves,

Have watched me rise from the darkness of
    war,
Dripping with my enemies' blood. I drove
420 Five great giants into chains, chased
All of that race from the earth. I swam
In the blackness of night, hunting monsters
Out of the ocean, and killing them one
By one; death was my errand and the fate
425 They had earned. Now Grendel and I are
    called
Together, and I've come. Grant me, then,
Lord and protector of this noble place,
A single request! I have come so far,
Oh shelterer of warriors and your people's
    loved friend,
430 That this one favor you should not refuse
    me—
That I, alone and with the help of my men,
May purge all evil from this hall. I have heard,
Too, that the monster's scorn of men
Is so great that he needs no weapons and fears
    none.
435 Nor will I. My lord Higlac
Might think less of me if I let my sword
Go where my feet were afraid to, if I hid
Behind some broad linden shield: my hands
Alone shall fight for me, struggle for life
440 Against the monster. God must decide
Who will be given to death's cold grip.
Grendel's plan, I think, will be
What it has been before, to invade this hall
And gorge his belly with our bodies. If he can,
445 If he can. And I think, if my time will have
    come,
There'll be nothing to mourn over, no corpse
    to prepare

For its grave: Grendel will carry our bloody
Flesh to the moors, crunch on our bones
And smear torn scraps of our skin on the walls
450 Of his den. No, I expect no Danes
Will fret about sewing our shrouds, if he wins.
And if death does take me, send the hammered
Mail of my armor to Higlac, return
The inheritance I had from Hrethel, and he
455 From Wayland.* Fate will unwind as it must!"

7

Hrothgar replied, protector of the Danes:
"Beowulf, you've come to us in friendship,
    and because
Of the reception your father found at our
    court.
Edgetho had begun a bitter feud,
460 Killing Hathlaf,* a Wulfing warrior:
Your father's countrymen were afraid of war,
If he returned to his home, and they turned
    him away.
Then he traveled across the curving waves
To the land of the Danes. I was new to the
    throne,
465 Then, a young man ruling this wide
Kingdom and its golden city: Hergar,
My older brother, a far better man
Than I, had died and dying made me,
Second among Healfdane's sons, first
470 In this nation. I bought the end of Edgetho's
Quarrel, sent ancient treasures through the
    ocean's

Furrows to the Wulfings;* your father swore
He'd keep that peace. My tongue grows heavy,
And my heart, when I try to tell you what
    Grendel
475 Has brought us, the damage he's done, here
In this hall. You see for yourself how much
    smaller
Our ranks have become, and can guess what
    we've lost
To his terror. Surely the Lord Almighty
Could stop his madness, smother his lust!
480 How many times have my men, glowing
With courage drawn from too many cups
Of ale, sworn to stay after dark
And stem that horror with a sweep of their
    swords.
And then, in the morning, this mead-hall
    glittering
485 With new light would be drenched with
    blood, the benches
Stained red, the floors, all wet from that fiend's
Savage assault—and my soldiers would be
    fewer
Still, death taking more and more.
But to table, Beowulf, a banquet in your
    honor:
490 Let us toast your victories, and talk of the
    future."
    Then Hrothgar's men gave places to the
    Geats,
Yielded benches to the brave visitors
And led them to the feast. The keeper of the
    mead
Came carrying out the carved flasks,
495 And poured that bright sweetness. A poet
Sang, from time to time, in a clear

Pure voice. Danes and visiting Geats
Celebrated as one, drank and rejoiced.

8

Unferth* spoke, Ecglaf's* son,
500 Who sat at Hrothgar's feet, spoke harshly
And sharp (vexed by Beowulf's adventure,
By their visitor's courage, and angry that
          anyone
In Denmark or anywhere on earth had ever
Acquired glory and fame greater
505 Than his own):
                    "You're Beowulf, are you—the
          same
Boastful fool who fought a swimming
Match with Brecca,* both of you daring
And young and proud, exploring the deepest
510 Seas, risking your lives for no reason
But the danger? All older and wiser heads
          warned you
Not to, but no one could check such pride.
With Brecca at your side you swam along
The sea-paths, your swift-moving hands
          pulling you
515 Over the ocean's face. Then winter
Churned through the water, the waves ran you
As they willed, and you struggled seven long
          nights
To survive. And at the end victory was his,
Not yours. The sea carried him close
520 To his home, to southern Norway, near

The land of the Brondings,* where he ruled
    and was loved,
Where his treasure was piled and his strength
    protected
His towns and his people. He'd promised to
    outswim you:
Bonstan's* son made that boast ring true.
525 You've been lucky in your battles, Beowulf,
    but I think
Your luck may change if you challenge
    Grendel,
Staying a whole night through in this hall,
Waiting where that fiercest of demons can
    find you."
    Beowulf answered, Edgetho's great son:
530   "Ah! Unferth, my friend, your face
Is hot with ale, and your tongue has tried
To tell us about Brecca's doings. But the truth
Is simple: no man swims in the sea
As I can, no strength is a match for mine.
535 As boys, Brecca and I had boasted—
We were both too young to know better—
    that we'd risk
Our lives far out at sea, and so
We did. Each of us carried a naked
Sword, prepared for whales or the swift
540 Sharp teeth and beaks of needlefish.
He could never leave me behind, swim faster
Across the waves than I could, and I
Had chosen to remain close to his side.
I remained near him for five long nights,
545 Until a flood swept us apart;
The frozen sea surged around me,
It grew dark, the wind turned bitter, blowing
From the north, and the waves were savage.
    Creatures

Who sleep deep in the sea were stirred
550 Into life—and the iron hammered links
Of my mail shirt, these shining bits of metal
Woven across my breast, saved me
From death. A monster seized me, drew me
Swiftly toward the bottom, swimming with its
        claws
555 Tight in my flesh. But fate let me
Find its heart with my sword, hack myself
Free; I fought that beast's last battle,
Left it floating lifeless in the sea.

9

    "Other monsters crowded around me,
560 Continually attacking. I treated them politely,
Offering the edge of my razor-sharp sword.
But the feast, I think, did not please them,
        filled
Their evil bellies with no banquet-rich food,
Thrashing there at the bottom of the sea;
565 By morning they'd decided to sleep on the
        shore,
Lying on their backs, their blood spilled out
On the sand. Afterwards, sailors could cross
That sea-road and feel no fear; nothing
Would stop their passing. Then God's bright
        beacon
570 Appeared in the east, the water lay still,
And at last I could see the land, wind-swept
Cliff-walls at the edge of the coast. Fate saves
The living when they drive away death by
        themselves!

Lucky or not, nine was the number

575 Of sea-huge monsters I killed. What man,
Anywhere under Heaven's high arch, has
fought
In such darkness, endured more misery or been
harder
Pressed? Yet I survived the sea, smashed
The monsters' hot jaws, swam home from my
journey.

580 The swift-flowing waters swept me along
And I landed on Finnish soil. I've heard
No tales of you, Unferth, telling
Of such clashing terror, such contests in the
night!
Brecca's battles were never so bold;

585 Neither he nor you can match me—and I mean
No boast, have announced no more than I
know
To be true. And there's more: you murdered
your brothers,
Your own close kin. Words and bright wit
Won't help your soul; you'll suffer hell's fires,

590 Unferth, forever tormented. Ecglaf's
Proud son, if your hands were as hard, your
heart
As fierce as you think it, no fool would dare
To raid your hall, ruin Herot
And oppress its prince, as Grendel has done.

595 But he's learned that terror is his alone,
Discovered he can come for your people with
no fear
Of reprisal; he's found no fighting, here,
But only food, only delight.
He murders as he likes, with no mercy, gorges

600 And feasts on your flesh, and expects no
trouble,

No quarrel from the quiet Danes. Now
The Geats will show him courage, soon
He can test his strength in battle. And when
    the sun
Comes up again, opening another
605   Bright day from the south, anyone in
    Denmark
May enter this hall: that evil will be gone!"
   Hrothgar, gray-haired and brave, sat
    happily
Listening, the famous ring-giver sure,
At last, that Grendel could be killed; he
    believed
610   In Beowulf's bold strength and the firmness
    of his spirit.
   There was the sound of laughter, and the
    cheerful clanking
Of cups, and pleasant words. Then Welthow,*
Hrothgar's gold-ringed queen, greeted
The warriors; a noble woman who knew
615   What was right, she raised a flowing cup
To Hrothgar first, holding it high
For the lord of the Danes to drink, wishing
    him
Joy in that feast. The famous king
Drank with pleasure and blessed their
    banquet.
620   Then Welthow went from warrior to warrior,
Pouring a portion from the jeweled cup
For each, till the bracelet-wearing queen
Had carried the mead-cup among them and it
    was Beowulf's
Turn to be served. She saluted the Geats'
625   Great prince, thanked God for answering her
    prayers,
For allowing her hands the happy duty

Of offering mead to a hero who would help
Her afflicted people. He drank what she
    poured,
Edgetho's brave son, then assured the Danish
630 Queen that his heart was firm and his hands
Ready:
        "When we crossed the sea, my
    comrades
And I, I already knew that all
My purpose was this: to win the good will
635 Of your people or die in battle, pressed
In Grendel's fierce grip. Let me live in
    greatness
And courage, or here in this hall welcome
My death!"
           Welthow was pleased with his
    words,
640 His bright-tongued boasts; she carried them
    back
To her lord, walked nobly across to his side.
   The feast went on, laughter and music
And the brave words of warriors celebrating
Their delight. Then Hrothgar rose, Healfdane's
645 Son, heavy with sleep; as soon
As the sun had gone, he knew that Grendel
Would come to Herot, would visit that hall
When night had covered the earth with its net
And the shapes of darkness moved black and
    silent
650 Through the world. Hrothgar's warriors rose
    with him.
   He went to Beowulf, embraced the Geats'
Brave prince, wished him well, and hoped
That Herot would be his to command. And
    then

He declared:

655   "No one strange to this land
Has ever been granted what I've given you,
No one in all the years of my rule.
Make this best of all mead-halls yours, and
     then
Keep it free of evil, fight
660 With glory in your heart! Purge Herot
And your ship will sail home with its
     treasure-holds full."

10

Then Hrothgar left that hall, the Danes'
Great protector, followed by his court; the
     queen
Had preceded him and he went to lie at her
     side,
665 Seek sleep near his wife. It was said that God
Himself had set a sentinel in Herot,
Brought Beowulf as a guard against Grendel
     and a shield
Behind whom the king could safely rest.
And Beowulf was ready, firm with our Lord's
670 High favor and his own bold courage and
     strength.
     He stripped off his mail shirt, his helmet,
     his sword
Hammered from the hardest iron, and
     handed
All his weapons and armor to a servant,
Ordered his war-gear guarded till morning.
675 And then, standing beside his bed,

He exclaimed:

                "Grendel is no braver, no stronger
Than I am! I could kill him with my sword; I shall not,
Easy as it would be. This fiend is a bold
680   And famous fighter, but his claws and teeth
Scratching at my shield, his clumsy fists
Beating at my sword blade, would be helpless. I will meet him
With my hands empty—unless his heart
Fails him, seeing a soldier waiting
685   Weaponless, unafraid. Let God in His wisdom
Extend His hand where He wills, reward
Whom He chooses!"

                Then the Geats' great chief dropped
His head to his pillow, and around him, as ready
690   As they could be, lay the soldiers who had crossed the sea
At his side, each of them sure that he was lost
To the home he loved, to the high-walled towns
And the friends he had left behind where both he
And they had been raised. Each thought of the Danes
695   Murdered by Grendel in a hall where Geats
And not Danes now slept. But God's dread loom
Was woven with defeat for the monster, good fortune
For the Geats; help against Grendel was with them,

And through the might of a single man
700 They would win. Who doubts that God in
    His wisdom
And strength holds the earth forever
In His hands? Out in the darkness the
    monster
Began to walk. The warriors slept
In that gabled hall where they hoped that He
705 Would keep them safe from evil, guard them
From death till the end of their days was
    determined
And the thread should be broken. But
    Beowulf lay wakeful,
Watching, waiting, eager to meet
His enemy, and angry at the thought of his
    coming.

11

710   Out from the marsh, from the foot of
        misty
Hills and bogs, bearing God's hatred,
Grendel came, hoping to kill
Anyone he could trap on this trip to high
    Herot.
He moved quickly through the cloudy night,
715 Up from his swampland, sliding silently
Toward that gold-shining hall. He had visited
    Hrothgar's
Home before, knew the way—
But never, before nor after that night,
Found Herot defended so firmly, his
    reception

720 So harsh. He journeyed, forever joyless,
    Straight to the door, then snapped it open,
    Tore its iron fasteners with a touch
    And rushed angrily over the threshold.
    He strode quickly across the inlaid
725 Floor, snarling and fierce: his eyes
    Gleamed in the darkness, burned with a
        gruesome
    Light. Then he stopped, seeing the hall
    Crowded with sleeping warriors, stuffed
    With rows of young soldiers resting together.
730 And his heart laughed, he relished the sight,
    Intended to tear the life from those bodies
    By morning; the monster's mind was hot
    With the thought of food and the feasting his
        belly
    Would soon know. But fate, that night,
        intended
735 Grendel to gnaw the broken bones
    Of his last human supper. Human
    Eyes were watching his evil steps,
    Waiting to see his swift hard claws.
    Grendel snatched at the first Geat
740 He came to, ripped him apart, cut
    His body to bits with powerful jaws,
    Drank the blood from his veins and bolted
    Him down, hands and feet; death
    And Grendel's great teeth came together,
745 Snapping life shut. Then he stepped to another
    Still body, clutched at Beowulf with his claws,
    Grasped at a strong-hearted wakeful sleeper
    —And was instantly seized himself, claws
    Bent back as Beowulf leaned up on one arm.
750   That shepherd of evil, guardian of crime,
    Knew at once that nowhere on earth
    Had he met a man whose hands were harder;

His mind was flooded with fear—but nothing
Could take his talons and himself from that
　　tight
755　Hard grip. Grendel's one thought was to run
From Beowulf, flee back to his marsh and
　　hide there:
This was a different Herot than the hall he
　　had emptied.
But Higlac's follower remembered his final
Boast and, standing erect, stopped
760　The monster's flight, fastened those claws
In his fists till they cracked, clutched Grendel
Closer. The infamous killer fought
For his freedom, wanting no flesh but retreat,
Desiring nothing but escape; his claws
765　Had been caught, he was trapped. That trip
　　to Herot
Was a miserable journey for the writhing
　　monster!
　　　The high hall rang, its roof boards swayed,
And Danes shook with terror. Down
The aisles the battle swept, angry
770　And wild. Herot trembled, wonderfully
Built to withstand the blows, the struggling
Great bodies beating at its beautiful walls;
Shaped and fastened with iron, inside
And out, artfully worked, the building
775　Stood firm. Its benches rattled, fell
To the floor, gold-covered boards grating
As Grendel and Beowulf battled across them.
Hrothgar's wise men had fashioned Herot
To stand forever; only fire,
780　They had planned, could shatter what such
　　skill had put
Together, swallow in hot flames such
　　splendor

Of ivory and iron and wood. Suddenly
The sounds changed, the Danes started
In new terror, cowering in their beds as the
      terrible
785   Screams of the Almighty's enemy sang
In the darkness, the horrible shrieks of pain
And defeat, the tears torn out of Grendel's
Taut throat, hell's captive caught in the arms
Of him who of all the men on earth
790   Was the strongest.

12

             That mighty protector of men
Meant to hold the monster till its life
Leaped out, knowing the fiend was no use
To anyone in Denmark. All of Beowulf's
795   Band had jumped from their beds, ancestral
Swords raised and ready, determined
To protect their prince if they could. Their
      courage
Was great but all wasted: they could hack at
      Grendel
From every side, trying to open
800   A path for his evil soul, but their points
Could not hurt him, the sharpest and hardest
      iron
Could not scratch at his skin, for that sin-
      stained demon
Had bewitched all men's weapons, laid spells
That blunted every mortal man's blade.
805   And yet his time had come, his days

Were over, his death near; down
To hell he would go, swept groaning and
    helpless
To the waiting hands of still worse fiends.
Now he discovered—once the afflictor
810 Of men, tormentor of their days—what it
    meant
To feud with Almighty God: Grendel
Saw that his strength was deserting him, his
    claws
Bound fast, Higlac's brave follower tearing at
His hands. The monster's hatred rose higher,
815 But his power had gone. He twisted in pain,
And the bleeding sinews deep in his shoulder
Snapped, muscle and bone split
And broke. The battle was over, Beowulf
Had been granted new glory: Grendel
    escaped,
820 But wounded as he was could flee to his den,
His miserable hole at the bottom of the
    marsh,
Only to die, to wait for the end
Of all his days. And after that bloody
Combat the Danes laughed with delight.
825 He who had come to them from across the
    sea,
Bold and strong-minded, had driven affliction
Off, purged Herot clean. He was happy,
Now, with that night's fierce work; the Danes
Had been served as he'd boasted he'd serve
    them; Beowulf,
830 A prince of the Geats, had killed Grendel,
Ended the grief, the sorrow, the suffering
Forced on Hrothgar's helpless people
By a bloodthirsty fiend, No Dane doubted

The victory, for the proof, hanging high
835 From the rafters where Beowulf had hung it,
       was the monster's
     Arm, claw and shoulder and all.

13

     And then, in the morning, crowds
       surrounded
     Herot, warriors coming to that hall
     From faraway lands, princes and leaders
840 Of men hurrying to behold the monster's
     Great staggering tracks. They gaped with no
       sense
     Of sorrow, felt no regret for his suffering,
     Went tracing his bloody footprints, his beaten
     And lonely flight, to the edge of the lake
845 Where he'd dragged his corpselike way,
       doomed
     And already weary of his vanishing life.
     The water was bloody, steaming and boiling
     In horrible pounding waves, heat
     Sucked from his magic veins; but the swirling
850 Surf had covered his death, hidden
     Deep in murky darkness his miserable
     End, as hell opened to receive him.
       Then old and young rejoiced, turned back
     From that happy pilgrimage, mounted their
       hard-hooved
855 Horses, high-spirited stallions, and rode them
     Slowly toward Herot again, retelling
     Beowulf's bravery as they jogged along.
     And over and over they swore that nowhere

On earth or under the spreading sky
860 Or between the seas, neither south nor north,
Was there a warrior worthier to rule over men.
(But no one meant Beowulf's praise to belittle
Hrothgar, their kind and gracious king!)
    And sometimes, when the path ran straight
        and clear,
865 They would let their horses race, red
And brown and pale yellow backs streaming
Down the road. And sometimes a proud old
        soldier
Who had heard songs of the ancient heroes
And could sing them all through, story after
        story,
870 Would weave a net of words for Beowulf's
Victory, tying the knot of his verses
Smoothly, swiftly, into place with a poet's
Quick skill, singing his new song aloud
While he shaped it, and the old songs as
        well—Siegmund's*
875 Adventures, familiar battles fought
By that glorious son of Vels.* And struggles,
Too, against evil and treachery that no one
Had ever heard of, that no one knew
Except Fitla,* who had fought at his uncle's
        side,
880 A brave young comrade carefully listening
When Siegmund's tongue unwound the
        wonders
He had worked, confiding in his closest friend.
There were tales of giants wiped from the
        earth
By Siegmund's might—and forever
        remembered,
885 Fame that would last him beyond life and
        death,

His daring battle with a treasure-rich dragon.
Heaving a hoary gray rock aside
Siegmund had gone down to the dragon
    alone,
Entered the hole where it hid and swung
890 His sword so savagely that it slit the creature
Through, pierced its flesh and pinned it
To a wall, hung it where his bright blade
    rested.
His courage and strength had earned him a
    king-like
Treasure, brought gold and rich rings to his
    glorious
895 Hands. He loaded that precious hoard
On his ship and sailed off with a shining
    cargo.
And the dragon dissolved in its own fierce
    blood.
    No prince, no protector of his warriors,
      knew power
And fame and glory like Siegmund's; his
    name
900 And his treasures grew great. Hermod* could
    have hoped
For at least as much; he was once the
    mightiest
Of men. But pride and defeat and betrayal
Sent him into exile with the Jutes,* and he
    ended
His life on their swords. That life had been
    misery
905 After misery, and he spread sorrow as long
As he lived it, heaped troubles on his
    unhappy people's
Heads, ignored all wise men's warnings,
Ruled only with courage. A king

Born, entrusted with ancient treasures
910 And cities full of stronghearted soldiers,
His vanity swelled him so vile and rank
That he could hear no voices but his own. He
  deserved
To suffer and die. But Beowulf was a prince
Well-loved, followed in friendship, not fear;
915 Hermod's heart had been hollowed by sin.
  The horses ran, when they could, on the
    gravel
Path. Morning slid past and was gone.
The whole brave company came riding to
  Herot,
Anxious to celebrate Beowulf's success
920 And stare at that arm. And Hrothgar rose
From beside his wife and came with his
  courtiers
Crowded around him. And Welthow rose
And joined him, his wife and queen with her
  women,
All of them walking to that wonderful hall.

14

925 Hrothgar stood at the top of the stairway
And stared at Grendel's great claw, swinging
High from that gold-shining roof. Then he
  cried:
  "Let God be thanked! Grendel's terrible
Anger hung over our heads too long,
930 Dropping down misery; but the Almighty
  makes miracles

When He pleases, wonder after wonder, and
    this world
Rests in His hands. I had given up hope,
Exhausted prayer, expected nothing
But misfortune forever. Herot was empty,
935   Bloody; the wisest and best of our people
Despaired as deeply, found hope no easier,
Knew nothing, no way to end this unequal
War of men and devils, warriors
And monstrous fiends. One man found it,
940   Came to Denmark and with the Lord's help
Did what none of the Danes could do,
Our wisdom, our strength, worthless without
    him.
The woman who bore him, whoever, wherever,
Alive now, or dead, knew the grace of the God
945   Of our fathers, was granted a son for her glory
And His. Beowulf, best of soldiers,
Let me take you to my heart, make you my son
    too,
And love you: preserve this passionate peace
Between us. And take, in return, whatever
950   You may want from whatever I own. Warriors
Deserving far less have been granted as much,
Given gifts and honored, though they fought
No enemy like yours. Glory is now yours
Forever and ever, your courage has earned it,
955   And your strength. May God be as good to
    you forever
As He has been to you here!"
                      Then Beowulf
    answered:
   "What we did was what our hearts helped
Our hands to perform; we came to fight
960   With Grendel, our strength against his. I wish

I could show you, here in Herot, his corpse
Stretched on this floor! I twisted my fingers
Around his claw, ripped and tore at it
As hard as I could: I meant to kill him
965 Right here, hold him so tightly that his heart
Would stop, would break, his life spill
On this floor. But God's will was against me,
As hard as I held him he still pulled free
And ran, escaped from this hall with the
        strength
970 Fear had given him. But he offered me his arm
And his claw, saved his life yet left me
That prize. And paying even so willingly
For his freedom he still fled with nothing
But the end of his evil days, ran
975 With death pressing at his back, pain
Splitting his panicked heart, pulling him
Step by step into hell. Let him burn
In torment, lying and trembling, waiting
For the brightness of God to bring him his
        reward."
980   Unferth grew quiet, gave up quarreling over
Beowulf's old battles, stopped all his boasting
Once everyone saw proof of that prince's
        strength,
Grendel's huge claw swinging high
From Hrothgar's mead-hall roof, the fingers
985 Of that loathsome hand ending in nails
As hard as bright steel—so hard, they all said,
That not even the sharpest of swords could
        have cut
It through, broken it off the monster's
Arm and ended its life, as Beowulf
990 Had done armed with only his bare hands.

15

Then the king ordered Herot cleaned
And hung with decorations: hundreds of
    hands,
Men and women, hurried to make
The great hall ready. Golden tapestries
995 Were lined along the walls, for a host
Of visitors to see and take pleasure in. But
    that glorious
Building was bent and broken, its iron
Hinges cracked and sprung from their corners
All around the hall. Only
1000 Its roof was undamaged when the blood-
    stained demon
Burst out of Herot, desperately breaking
Beowulf's grip, running wildly
From what no one escapes, struggle and
    writhe
As he will. Wanting to stay we go,
1005 All beings here on God's earth, wherever
It is written that we go, taking our bodies
From death's cold bed to the unbroken sleep
That follows life's feast.
                        Then Hrothgar made
    his way
1010 To the hall; it was time, and his heart drew
    him
To the banquet. No victory was celebrated
    better,
By more or by better men and their king.
A mighty host, and famous, they lined
The benches, rejoicing; the king and Hrothulf,*
1015 His nephew, toasted each other, raised mead-
    cups

High under Herot's great roof, their speech
Courteous and warm. King and people
Were one; none of the Danes was plotting,
Then, no treachery hid in their smiles.
1020   Healfdane's son gave Beowulf a golden
Banner, a fitting flag to signal
His victory, and gave him, as well, a helmet,
And a coat of mail, and an ancient sword;
They were brought to him while the warriors
    watched. Beowulf
1025 Drank to those presents, not ashamed to be
    praised,
Richly rewarded in front of them all.
No ring-giver has given four such gifts,
Passed such treasures through his hands, with
    the grace
And warmth that Hrothgar showed. The
    helmet's
1030 Brim was wound with bands of metal,
Rounded ridges to protect whoever
Wore it from swords swung in the fiercest
Battles, shining iron edges
In hostile hands. And then the protector
1035 Of warriors, lord of the Danes, ordered
Eight horses led to the hall, and into it,
Eight steeds with golden bridles. One stood
With a jeweled saddle on its back, carved
Like the king's war-seat it was; it had carried
1040 Hrothgar when that great son of Healfdane
    rode
To war—and each time carried him wherever
The fighting was most fierce, and his
    followers had fallen.
Then Beowulf had been honored by both the
    gifts

Hrothgar could have given him, horses and
    weapons:
1045   The king commanded him to use them well.
Thus that guardian of Denmark's treasures
Had repaid a battle fought for his people
By giving noble gifts, had earned praise
For himself from those who try to know
    truth.

16

1050   And more: the lord of Herot ordered
Treasure-gifts for each of the Geats
Who'd sailed with Beowulf and still sat
    beside him,
Ancient armor and swords—and for the one
Murdered by Grendel gold was carefully
1055   Paid. The monster would have murdered
    again
And again had not God, and the hero's
    courage,
Turned fate aside. Then and now
Men must lie in their Maker's holy
Hands, moved only as He wills:
1060   Our hearts must seek out that will. The
    world,
And its long days full of labor, brings good
And evil; all who remain here meet both.
    Hrothgar's hall resounded with the harp's
High call, with songs and laughter and the
    telling
1065   Of tales, stories sung by the court

Poet as the joyful Danes drank
And listened, seated along their mead-benches.
He told them of Finn's* people, attacking
Hnaf* with no warning, half wiping out

1070 That Danish tribe, and killing its king.
Finn's wife, Hnaf's sister, learned what good
            faith
Was worth to her husband: his honeyed words
And treachery cost her two belovèd lives,
Her son and her brother, both falling on spears

1075 Guided by fate's hand. How she wept!
And when morning came she had reason to
            mourn,
To weep for her dead, her slaughtered son
And the bloody corpse of his uncle—both
The men she most dearly loved, and whose
            love

1080 She could trust to protect her. But Finn's
            troops, too,
Had fallen to Danish spears: too few
Were left to drive the Danes to their death,
To force Hnaf's follower, Hengest,* to flee
The hall where they'd fought and he'd stayed.
            Finn offered them,

1085 Instead of more war, words of peace:
There would be no victory, they'd divide the
            hall
And the throne, half to the Danes, half
To Finn's followers. When gifts were given
Finn would give Hengest and his soldiers half,

1090 Share shining rings, silver
And gold, with the Danes, both sides equal,
All of them richer, all of their purses
Heavy, every man's heart warm
With the comfort of gold.

1095   Both sides accepted

Peace and agreed to keep it. Finn
Swore it with solemn oaths: what wise men
Had written was his word as well as theirs.
He and the brave Hengest would live
1100 Like brothers; neither leader nor led would
 break
The truce, would not talk of evil things,
Remind the Danes that the man they served
Killed Hnaf, their lord. They had no king,
And no choice. And he swore that his sword
 would silence
1105 Wagging tongues if Frisian* warriors
Stirred up hatred, brought back the past.
 A funeral pyre was prepared, and gold
Was brought; Hnaf's dead body was dressed
For burning, and the others with him. Bloody
1110 Mail shirts could be seen, and golden helmets,
Some carved with boar-heads, all battle-hard
And as useless, now, as the corpses that still
 wore them,
Soldier after soldier! Then Hnaf's sister,
Finn's sad wife, gave her son's body
1115 To be burned in that fire; the flames charring
His uncle would consume both kinsmen at
 once.
Then she wept again, and weeping sang
The dead's last praise. The Danish king
Was lifted into place, smoke went curling
1120 Up, logs roared, open
Wounds split and burst, skulls
Melted, blood came bubbling down,
And the greedy fire-demons drank flesh and
 bones
From the dead of both sides, until nothing was
 left.

1125   Finn released a few of his soldiers,
        Allowed them to return to their distant towns
        And estates. Hengest lived the whole stormy
        Winter through, there with Finn
        Whom he hated. But his heart lived in
            Denmark—
1130   Which he and the other survivors could not
            visit,
        Could not sail to, as long as the wind-
            whipped sea
        Crashed and whirled, or while winter's cold
            hands
        Froze the water hard, tied it
        In icy knots. They would wait for the new
            year,
1135   For spring to come following the sun, melting
        The old year away and reopening the ocean.
        Winter was over, the earth grew lovely,
        And Hengest dreamed of his home—but
            revenge
        Came first, settling his bitter feud
1140   With Finn, whose bloody sword he could
            never
        Forget. He planned, he waited, wove plans
        And waited. Then a Danish warrior dropped
        A sword in his lap, a weapon Finn
        And his men remembered and feared, and the
            time
1145   Had come, and Hengest rose, hearing
        The Danes' murmur, and drove his new
            sword
        Into Finn's belly, butchering that king
        Under his own roof. And the Danes rose,

Their hearts full of Finn's treachery,
1150 And the misery he'd brought them, their
    sword arms restless
And eager. The hall they'd shared with their
    enemies
Ran red with enemy blood and bodies
Rolled on the floor beside Finn. They took
The queen, looted everything they could find
1155 That belonged to her dead husband, loaded
Their ship with rings, necklaces, shining
Jewels wonderfully worked, and sailed
Bringing treasure and a willing captive to the
    land
She'd left and had longed for, alone no longer.
1160   The singer finished his song; his listeners
Laughed and drank, their pleasure loud
In that hall. The cup-bearers hurried with
    their sparkling
Vessels. And then the queen, Welthow,
    wearing her bright crown,
Appeared among them, came to Hrothgar and
    Hrothulf, his nephew,
1165 Seated peacefully together, their friendship and
    Hrothulf's good faith still unbroken.
And Unferth sat at Hrothgar's feet; everyone
    trusted him,
Believed in his courage, although he'd spilled
    his relatives' blood.
Then Welthow spoke:
                    "Accept this cup,
1170 My lord and king! May happiness come
To the Danes' great ring-giver; may the Geats
    receive
Mild words from your mouth, words they
    have earned!
Let gifts flow freely from your open hands,

Treasures your armies have brought you from
    all over
1175   The world. I have heard that the greatest of
    the Geats
Now rests in your heart like a son. Herot
Stands purged, restored by his strength:
    celebrate
His courage, rejoice and be generous while a
    kingdom
Sits in your palm, a people and power
1180   That death will steal. But your sons will be
    safe,
Sheltered in Hrothulf's gracious protection,
If fate takes their father while Hrothulf is
    alive;
I know your nephew's kindness, I know
He'll repay in kind the goodness you have
    shown him,
1185   Support your two young sons as you
And I sustained him in his own early days,
His father dead and he but a boy."
    Then she walked to the bench where
        Hrethric* and Hrothmund,*
Her two sons, sat together; Beowulf,
1190   Prince of the Geats, was seated between them;
Crossing the hall she sat quietly at their side.

18

    They brought a foaming cup and offered it
To Beowulf; it was taken and given in
    friendship.

And he was given a mail shirt, and golden
    armbands,
1195 And the most beautiful necklace known to
    men:
Nowhere in any treasure-hoard anywhere
On earth was there anything like it, not since
Hama* carried the Brosings'* necklace
Home to his glorious city, saved
1200 Its tight-carved jewels, and his skin, and his
    soul
From Ermric's* treachery, and then came to
    God.
Higlac had it next, Swerting's*
Grandson; defending the golden hoard
His battle-hard hands had won for him, the
    Geats'
1205 Proud king lost it, was carried away
By fate when too much pride made him feud
With the Frisians. He had asked for misery;
    it was granted him.
He'd borne those precious stones on a ship's
Broad back; he fell beneath his shield.
1210 His body, and his shining coat of mail,
And that necklace, all lay for Franks* to
    pluck,
For jackal warriors to find when they walked
    through
The rows of corpses; Geats, and their king,
Lay slaughtered wherever the robbers looked.
1215   The warriors shouted. And Welthow
    spoke:
  "Wear these bright jewels, belovèd
    Beowulf;
Enjoy them, and the rings, and the gold, oh
    fortunate young

Warrior; grow richer, let your fame and your
    strength
Go hand in hand; and lend these two boys
1220 Your wise and gentle heart! I'll remember your
Kindness. Your glory is too great to forget:
It will last forever, wherever the earth
Is surrounded by the sea, the winds' home,
And waves lap at its walls. Be happy
1225 For as long as you live! Your good fortune
    warms
My soul. Spread your blessèd protection
Across my son, and my king's son!
All men speak softly, here, speak mildly
And trust their neighbors, protect their lord,
1230 Are loyal followers who would fight as joyfully
As they drink. May your heart help you do as I
    ask!"
    She returned to her seat. The soldiers ate
And drank like kings. The savage fate
Decreed for them hung dark and unknown,
    what would follow
1235 After nightfall, when Hrothgar withdrew from
    the hall,
Sought his bed and left his soldiers
To theirs. Herot would house a host
Of men, that night, as it had been meant to do.
They stacked away the benches, spread out
1240 Blankets and pillows. But those beer-drinking
    sleepers
Lay down with death beside their beds.
They slept with their shining shields at the edge
Of their pillows; the hall was filled with helmets
Hanging near motionless heads; spears
1245 Stood by their hands, their hammered mail
    shirts
Covered their chests. It was the Danes' custom

To be ready for war, wherever they rested,
At home or in foreign lands, at their lord's
Quick call if he needed them, if trouble came
1250 To their king. They knew how soldiers must
live!

19

They sank into sleep. The price of that
evening's
Rest was too high for the Dane who bought it
With his life, paying as others had paid
When Grendel inhabited Herot, the hall
1255 His till his crimes pulled him into hell.
And now it was known that a monster had
died
But a monster still lived, and meant revenge.
She'd brooded on her loss, misery had brewed
In her heart, that female horror, Grendel's
1260 Mother, living in the murky cold lake
Assigned her since Cain had killed his only
Brother, slain his father's son
With an angry sword. God drove him off,
Outlawed him to the dry and barren desert,
1265 And branded him with a murderer's mark. And
he bore
A race of fiends accursed like their father;
So Grendel was drawn to Herot, an outcast
Come to meet the man who awaited him.
He'd snatched at Beowulf's arm, but that
prince
1270 Remembered God's grace and the strength
He'd given him

And relied on the Lord for all the help,
The comfort and support he would need. He
    killed
The monster, as God had meant him to do,
Tore the fiend apart and forced him
1275 To run as rapidly as he could toward death's
Cold waiting hands. His mother's sad heart,
And her greed, drove her from her den on the
    dangerous
Pathway of revenge.

                    So she reached Herot,
1280 Where the Danes slept as though already
    dead;
Her visit ended their good fortune, reversed
The bright vane of their luck. No female, no
    matter
How fierce, could have come with a man's
    strength,
Fought with the power and courage men
    fight with,
1285 Smashing their shining swords, their bloody,
Hammer-forged blades onto boar-headed
    helmets,
Slashing and stabbing with the sharpest of
    points.
The soldiers raised their shields and drew
Those gleaming swords, swung them above
1290 The piled-up benches, leaving their mail
    shirts
And their helmets where they'd lain when the
    terror took hold of them.
To save her life she moved still faster,
Took a single victim and fled from the hall,
Running to the moors, discovered, but her
    supper
1295 Assured, sheltered in her dripping claws.

She'd taken Hrothgar's closest friend,
The man he most loved of all men on earth;
She'd killed a glorious soldier, cut
A noble life short. No Geat could have
      stopped her:
1300 Beowulf and his band had been given better
Beds; sleep had come to them in a different
Hall. Then all Herot burst into shouts:
She had carried off Grendel's claw. Sorrow
Had returned to Denmark. They'd traded
      deaths,
1305 Danes and monsters, and no one had won,
Both had lost!
              The wise old king
Trembled in anger and grief, his dearest
Friend and adviser dead. Beowulf
1310 Was sent for at once: a messenger went
      swiftly
To his rooms and brought him. He came, his
      band
About him, as dawn was breaking through,
The best of all warriors, walking to where
      Hrothgar
Sat waiting, the gray-haired king wondering
1315 If God would ever end this misery.
The Geats tramped quickly through the hall;
      their steps
Beat and echoed in the silence. Beowulf
Rehearsed the words he would want with
      Hrothgar;
He'd ask the Danes' great lord if all
1320 Were at peace, if the night had passed quietly.

20

Hrothgar answered him, protector of his
    people:
"There's no happiness to ask about!
    Anguish has descended
On the Danes. Esher* is dead, Ermlaf's*
Older brother and my own most trusted
1325   Counselor and friend, my comrade, when we
    went
Into battle, who'd beaten back enemy swords,
Standing at my side. All my soldiers
Should be as he was, their hearts as brave
And as wise! Another wandering fiend
1330   Has found him in Herot, murdered him, fled
With his corpse: he'll be eaten, his flesh
    become
A horrible feast—and who knows where
The beast may be hiding, its belly stuffed full?
She's taking revenge for your victory over
    Grendel,
1335   For your strength, your mighty grip, and that
    monster's
Death. For years he'd been preying on my
    people;
You came, he was dead in a single day,
And now there's another one, a second hungry
Fiend, determined to avenge the first,
1340   A monster willing and more than able
To bring us more sorrow—or so it must seem
To the many men mourning that noble
Treasure-giver, for all men were treated
Nobly by those hands now forever closed.
1345   "I've heard that my people, peasants
    working

In the fields, have seen a pair of such fiends
Wandering in the moors and marshes, giant
Monsters living in those desert lands.
And they've said to my wise men that, as
    well as they could see,
1350 One of the devils was a female creature.
The other, they say, walked through the
    wilderness
Like a man—but mightier than any man.
They were frightened, and they fled, hoping
    to find help
In Herot. They named the huge one Grendel:
1355 If he had a father no one knew him,
Or whether there'd been others before these
    two,
Hidden evil before hidden evil.
They live in secret places, windy
Cliffs, wolf-dens where water pours
1360 From the rocks, then runs underground,
    where mist
Steams like black clouds, and the groves of
    trees
Growing out over their lake are all covered
With frozen spray, and wind down snakelike
Roots that reach as far as the water
1365 And help keep it dark. At night that lake
Burns like a torch. No one knows its bottom,
No wisdom reaches such depths. A deer,
Hunted through the woods by packs of
    hounds,
A stag with great horns, though driven
    through the forest
1370 From faraway places, prefers to die
On those shores, refuses to save its life
In that water. It isn't far, nor is it
A pleasant spot! When the wind stirs

And storms, waves splash toward the sky,
1375 As dark as the air, as black as the rain
That the heavens weep. Our only help,
Again, lies with you. Grendel's mother
Is hidden in her terrible home, in a place
You've not seen. Seek it, if you dare! Save us,
1380 Once more, and again twisted gold,
Heaped-up ancient treasure, will reward you
For the battle you win!"

21

Beowulf spoke:
"Let your sorrow end! It is better for us all
1385 To avenge our friends, not mourn them
forever.
Each of us will come to the end of this life
On earth; he who can earn it should fight
For the glory of his name; fame after death
Is the noblest of goals. Arise, guardian
1390 Of this kingdom, let us go, as quickly as we
can,
And have a look at this lady monster.
I promise you this: she'll find no shelter,
No hole in the ground, no towering tree,
No deep bottom of a lake, where her sins can
hide.
1395 Be patient for one more day of misery;
I ask for no longer."
The old king leaped
To his feet, gave thanks to God for such
words.
Then Hrothgar's horse was brought, saddled

1400 And bridled. The Danes' wise ruler rode,
Stately and splendid; shield-bearing soldiers
Marched at his side. The monster's tracks
Led them through the forest; they followed
her heavy
Feet, that had swept straight across
1405 The shadowy waste land, her burden the
lifeless
Body of the best of Hrothgar's men.
The trail took them up towering, rocky
Hills, and over narrow, winding
Paths they had never seen, down steep
1410 And slippery cliffs where creatures from deep
In the earth hid in their holes. Hrothgar
Rode in front, with a few of his most
knowing
Men, to find their way. Then suddenly,
Where clumps of trees bent across
1415 Cold gray stones, they came to a dismal
Wood; below them was the lake, its water
Bloody and bubbling. And the Danes
shivered,
Miserable, mighty men tormented
By grief, seeing, there on that cliff
1420 Above the water, Esher's bloody
Head. They looked down at the lake, felt
How its heat rose up, watched the waves'
Blood-stained swirling. Their battle horns
sounded,
Then sounded again. Then they set down
their weapons.
1425   They could see the water crawling with
snakes,
Fantastic serpents swimming in the boiling
Lake, and sea beasts lying on the rocks
—The kind that infest the ocean, in the early

Dawn, often ending some ship's
1430 Journey with their wild jaws. They rushed
Angrily out of sight, when the battle horns
blew.
Beowulf aimed an arrow at one
Of the beasts, swimming sluggishly away,
And the point pierced its hide, stabbed
1435 To its heart; its life leaked out, death
Swept it off. Quickly, before
The dying monster could escape, they hooked
Its thrashing body with their curved boar-
spears,
Fought it to land, drew it up on the bluff,
1440 Then stood and stared at the incredible wave-
roamer,
Covered with strange scales and horrible.
Then Beowulf
Began to fasten on his armor,
Not afraid for his life but knowing the woven
Mail, with its hammered links, could save
1445 That life when he lowered himself into the
lake,
Keep slimy monsters' claws from snatching at
His heart, preserve him for the battle he was
sent
To fight. Hrothgar's helmet would defend
him;
That ancient, shining treasure, encircled
1450 With hard-rolled metal, set there by some
smith's
Long dead hand, would block all battle
Swords, stop all blades from cutting at him
When he'd swum toward the bottom, gone
down in the surging
Water, deep toward the swirling sands.
1455 And Unferth helped him, Hrothgar's courtier

Lent him a famous weapon, a fine,
Hilted old sword named Hrunting;* it had
An iron blade, etched and shining
And hardened in blood. No one who'd worn it
1460 Into battle, swung it in dangerous places,
Daring and brave, had ever been deserted—
Nor was Beowulf's journey the first time it
     was taken
To an enemy's camp, or asked to support
Some hero's courage and win him glory.
1465 Unferth had tried to forget his greeting
To Beowulf, his drunken speech of welcome;
A mighty warrior, he lent his weapon
To a better one. Only Beowulf would risk
His life in that lake; Unferth was afraid,
1470 Gave up that chance to work wonders, win
     glory
And a hero's fame. But Beowulf and fear
Were strangers; he stood ready to dive into
     battle.

22

Then Edgetho's brave son spoke:
                         "Remember,
1475 Hrothgar, Oh knowing king, now
When my danger is near, the warm words we
     uttered,
And if your enemy should end my life
Then be, oh generous prince, forever
The father and protector of all whom I leave
1480 Behind me, here in your hands, my belovèd
Comrades left with no leader, their leader

Dead. And the precious gifts you gave me,
My friend, send them to Higlac. May he see
In their golden brightness, the Geats' great
    lord
1485 Gazing at your treasure, that here in Denmark
I found a noble protector, a giver
Of rings whose rewards I won and briefly
Relished. And you, Unferth, let
My famous old sword stay in your hands:
1490 I shall shape glory with Hrunting, or death
Will hurry me from this earth!"

                    As his words ended
He leaped into the lake, would not wait for
    anyone's
Answer; the heaving water covered him
1495 Over. For hours he sank through the waves;
At last he saw the mud of the bottom.
And all at once the greedy she-wolf
Who'd ruled those waters for half a hundred
Years discovered him, saw that a creature
1500 From above had come to explore the bottom
Of her wet world. She welcomed him in her
    claws,
Clutched at him savagely but could not harm
    him,
Tried to work her fingers through the tight
Ring-woven mail on his breast, but tore
1505 And scratched in vain. Then she carried him,
    armor
And sword and all, to her home; he struggled
To free his weapon, and failed. The fight
Brought other monsters swimming to see
Her catch, a host of sea beasts who beat at
1510 His mail shirt, stabbing with tusks and teeth
As they followed along. Then he realized,
    suddenly,

That she'd brought him into someone's
     battle-hall,
And there the water's heat could not hurt him,
Nor anything in the lake attack him through
1515 The building's high-arching roof. A brilliant
Light burned all around him, the lake
Itself like a fiery flame.
                         Then he saw
The mighty water witch, and swung his
     sword,
1520 His ring-marked blade, straight at her head;
The iron sang its fierce song,
Sang Beowulf's strength. But her guest
Discovered that no sword could slice her evil
Skin, that Hrunting could not hurt her, was
     useless
1525 Now when he needed it. They wrestled, she
     ripped
And tore and clawed at him, bit holes in his
     helmet,
And that too failed him; for the first time in
     years
Of being worn to war it would earn no glory;
It was the last time anyone would wear it. But
     Beowulf
1530 Longed only for fame, leaped back
Into battle. He tossed his sword aside,
Angry; the steel-edged blade lay where
He'd dropped it. If weapons were useless he'd
     use
His hands, the strength in his fingers. So fame
1535 Comes to the men who mean to win it
And care about nothing else! He raised
His arms and seized her by the shoulder;
     anger

Doubled his strength, he threw her to the floor.
She fell, Grendel's fierce mother, and the Geats'
1540 Proud prince was ready to leap on her. But she
      rose
At once and repaid him with her clutching
      claws,
Wildly tearing at him. He was weary, that best
And strongest of soldiers; his feet stumbled
And in an instant she had him down, held
      helpless.
1545 Squatting with her weight on his stomach, she
      drew
A dagger, brown with dried blood, and
      prepared
To avenge her only son. But he was stretched
On his back, and her stabbing blade was
      blunted
By the woven mail shirt he wore on his chest.
1550 The hammered links held; the point
Could not touch him. He'd have traveled to
      the bottom of the earth,
Edgetho's son, and died there, if that shining
Woven metal had not helped—and Holy
God, who sent him victory, gave judgment
1555 For truth and right, Ruler of the Heavens,
Once Beowulf was back on his feet and
      fighting.

23

Then he saw, hanging on the wall, a heavy
Sword, hammered by giants, strong
And blessed with their magic, the best of all
    weapons
1560 But so massive that no ordinary man could
    lift
Its carved and decorated length. He drew it
From its scabbard, broke the chain on its hilt,
And then, savage, now, angry
And desperate, lifted it high over his head
1565 And struck with all the strength he had left,
Caught her in the neck and cut it through,
Broke bones and all. Her body fell
To the floor, lifeless, the sword was wet
With her blood, and Beowulf rejoiced at the
    sight.
1570   The brilliant light shone, suddenly,
As though burning in that hall, and as bright
    as Heaven's
Own candle, lit in the sky. He looked
At her home, then following along the wall
Went walking, his hands tight on the sword,
1575 His heart still angry. He was hunting another
Dead monster, and took his weapon with him
For final revenge against Grendel's vicious
Attacks, his nighttime raids, over
And over, coming to Herot when Hrothgar's
1580 Men slept, killing them in their beds,
Eating some on the spot, fifteen
Or more, and running to his loathsome moor
With another such sickening meal waiting
In his pouch. But Beowulf repaid him for
    those visits,

1585 Found him lying dead in his corner,
Armless, exactly as that fierce fighter
Had sent him out from Herot, then struck off
His head with a single swift blow. The body
Jerked for the last time, then lay still.

1590   The wise old warriors who surrounded
        Hrothgar,
Like him staring into the monsters' lake,
Saw the waves surging and blood
Spurting through. They spoke about Beowulf,
All the graybeards, whispered together

1595 And said that hope was gone, that the hero
Had lost fame and his life at once, and would
    never
Return to the living, come back as triumphant
As he had left; almost all agreed that Grendel's
Mighty mother, the she-wolf, had killed him.

1600 The sun slid over past noon, went further
Down. The Danes gave up, left
The lake and went home, Hrothgar with them.
The Geats stayed, sat sadly, watching,
Imagining they saw their lord but not believing
They would ever see him again.

1605   —Then the sword
Melted, blood-soaked, dripping down
Like water, disappearing like ice when the
    world's
Eternal Lord loosens invisible
Fetters and unwinds icicles and frost

1610 As only He can, He who rules
Time and seasons, He who is truly
God. The monsters' hall was full of
Rich treasures, but all that Beowulf took
Was Grendel's head and the hilt of the giants'

1615 Jeweled sword; the rest of that ring-marked
Blade had dissolved in Grendel's steaming

Blood, boiling even after his death.
And then the battle's only survivor
Swam up and away from those silent corpses;
1620 The water was calm and clean, the whole
Huge lake peaceful once the demons who'd
      lived in it
Were dead.
          Then that noble protector of all
      seamen
Swam to land, rejoicing in the heavy
1625 Burdens he was bringing with him. He
And all his glorious band of Geats
Thanked God that their leader had come
      back unharmed;
They left the lake together. The Geats
Carried Beowulf's helmet, and his mail shirt.
1630 Behind them the water slowly thickened
As the monsters' blood came seeping up.
They walked quickly, happily, across
Roads all of them remembered, left
The lake and the cliffs alongside it, brave men
1635 Staggering under the weight of Grendel's skull,
Too heavy for fewer than four of them to
      handle—
Two on each side of the spear jammed through
      it—
Yet proud of their ugly load and determined
That the Danes, seated in Herot, should see it.
1640 Soon, fourteen Geats arrived
At the hall, bold and warlike, and with
      Beowulf,
Their lord and leader, they walked on the
      mead-hall
Green. Then the Geats' brave prince entered
Herot, covered with glory for the daring
1645 Battles he had fought; he sought Hrothgar

To salute him and show Grendel's head.
He carried that terrible trophy by the hair,
Brought it straight to where the Danes sat,
Drinking, the queen among them. It was a
    weird
1650 And wonderful sight, and the warriors stared.

24

Beowulf spoke:
        "Hrothgar! Behold,
Great Healfdane's son, this glorious sign
Of victory, brought you by joyful Geats.
1655 My life was almost lost, fighting for it,
Struggling under water: I'd have been dead at
    once,
And the fight finished, the she-devil
    victorious,
If our Father in Heaven had not helped me.
    Hrunting,
Unferth's noble weapon, could do nothing,
1660 Nor could I, until the Ruler of the world
Showed me, hanging shining and beautiful
On a wall, a mighty old sword—so God
Gives guidance to those who can find it from
    no one
Else. I used the weapon He had offered me,
1665 Drew it and, when I could, swung it, killed
The monstrous hag in her own home.
Then the ring-marked blade burned away,
As that boiling blood spilled out. I carried
Off all that was left, this hilt.

1670 I've avenged their crimes, and the Danes
      they've killed.
    And I promise you that whoever sleeps in
      Herot
    —You, your brave soldiers, anyone
    Of all the people in Denmark, old
    Or young—they, and you, may now sleep
1675 Without fear of either monster, mother
    Or son."
               Then he gave the golden sword hilt
    To Hrothgar, who held it in his wrinkled hands
    And stared at what giants had made, and
      monsters
1680 Owned; it was his, an ancient weapon
    Shaped by wonderful smiths, now that Grendel
    And his evil mother had been driven from the
      earth,
    God's enemies scattered and dead. That best
    Of swords belonged to the best of Denmark's
1685 Rulers, the wisest ring-giver Danish
    Warriors had ever known. The old king
    Bent close to the handle of the ancient relic,
    And saw written there the story of ancient
      wars
    Between good and evil, the opening of the
      waters,
1690 The Flood sweeping giants away, how they
      suffered
    And died, that race who hated the Ruler
    Of us all and received judgment from His
      hands,
    Surging waves that found them wherever
    They fled. And Hrothgar saw runic letters
1695 Clearly carved in that shining hilt,
    Spelling its original owner's name,

He for whom it was made, with its twisted
Handle and snakelike carvings. Then he spoke,
Healfdane's son, and everyone was silent.
1700   "What I say, speaking from a full memory
And after a life spent in seeking
What was right for my people, is this: this
          prince
Of the Geats, Beowulf, was born a better
Man! Your fame is everywhere, my friend,
1705   Reaches to the ends of the earth, and you hold
          it in your heart wisely,
Patient with your strength and our weakness.
          What I said I will do, I will do,
In the name of the friendship we've sworn.
          Your strength must solace your people,
Now, and mine no longer.
                              "Be not
1710   As Hermod once was to my people, too proud
To care what their hearts hid, bringing them
Only destruction and slaughter. In his mad
Rages he killed them himself, comrades
And followers who ate at his table. At the end
1715   He was alone, knew none of the joys of life
With other men, a famous ruler
Granted greater strength than anyone
Alive in his day but dark and bloodthirsty
In spirit. He shared out no treasure, showed
1720   His soldiers no road to riches and fame.
And then that affliction on his people's face
Suffered horribly for his sins. Be taught
By his lesson, learn what a king must be:
I tell his tale, old as I am,
1725   Only for you.
                    "Our eternal Lord
Grants some men wisdom, some wealth, makes
          others

Great. The world is God's, He allows
A man to grow famous, and his family rich,
1730 Gives him land and towns to rule
And delight in, lets his kingdom reach
As far as the world runs—and who
In human unwisdom, in the middle of such
power,
Remembers that it all will end, and too soon?
1735 Prosperity, prosperity, prosperity: nothing
Troubles him, no sickness, not passing time,
No sorrows, no sudden war breaking
Out of nowhere, but all the world turns
When he spins it. How can he know when he
sins?

25

1740 "And then pride grows in his heart, planted
Quietly but flourishing. And while the keeper
of his soul
Sleeps on, while conscience rests and the world
Turns faster a murderer creeps closer, comes
carrying
A tight-strung bow with terrible arrows.
1745 And those sharp points strike home, are shot
In his breast, under his helmet. He's helpless.
And so the Devil's dark urgings wound him,
for he can't
Remember how he clung to the rotting wealth
Of this world, how he clawed to keep it, how
he earned
1750 No honor, no glory, in giving golden
Rings, how he forgot the future glory

God gave him at his birth, and forgetting did
    not care.
And finally his body fails him, these bones
And flesh quickened by God fall
1755 And die—and some other soul inherits
His place in Heaven, some open-handed
Giver of old treasures, who takes no delight
In mere gold. Guard against such wickedness,
Belovèd Beowulf, best of warriors,
1760 And choose, instead, eternal happiness;
Push away pride! Your strength, your power,
Are yours for how many years? Soon
You'll return them where they came from,
    sickness or a sword's edge
Will end them, or a grasping fire, or the flight
1765 Of a spear, or surging waves, or a knife's
Bite, or the terror of old age, or your eyes
Darkening over. It will come, death
Comes faster than you think, no one can flee it.
    "So I have led the Danes for half
1770 A hundred years, protected them from all
    peoples
On this earth, my sword and my spear so ready
That no one anywhere under God's high sun
Was eager to wage war here in Denmark.
And here, here too the change has come,
1775 And we wept for our dead when Grendel
    invaded
Herot, my enemy raided this hall;
My sorrow, my grief, was as great and lasting
As it was helpless. Then thanks be given to
    God,
Eternal Lord of us all: you came
1780 And that endless misery was over and I lived,
Now, to behold this bloody head!

Go in, go in: feast, be as happy
As your fame deserves. When morning shines
We shall each have owned more of my
        treasures."
1785   Beowulf obeyed him, entered Herot
Cheerfully and took his place at the table.
And once again Danes and Geats
Feasted together, a host of famous
Warriors in a single hall.—Then the web
1790 Of darkness fell and it was night. They rose;
Hrothgar, the gray-haired old Dane, was
        heavy
With sleep. And Beowulf was glad that a bed
Was waiting, the bravest of warriors
        exhausted
With the work he'd done. A Danish servant
1795 Showed him the road to that far-off, quiet
Country where sleep would come and take
        him
And his followers; Hrothgar's visitors were
        well
Cared for, whatever they needed was theirs.
        Then Beowulf rested; Herot rose high
1800 Above him, gleaming in the darkness; the
        Geats
Slept till a black-feathered raven sang
His cheerful song and the shining sun
Burned away shadows. And those seafarers
        hurried
From their beds, anxious to begin the voyage
1805 Home, ready to start, their hearts
Already sailing on a ship's swift back.
        Then Unferth came, with Hrunting, his
        famous
Sword, and offered it to Beowulf, asked him

To accept a precious gift. The prince
1810　Took it, thanked him, and declared the
　　　　weapon
One he was proud to own; his words
Blamed it for nothing, were spoken like the
　　　　hero
He was! The war-gear was ready, the Geats
Were armored and eager to be gone. Quickly,
1815　Beowulf sought Hrothgar's throne, where the
　　　　king
Sat waiting for his famous visitor's farewell.

26

Beowulf spoke:
　　　　　　　　"We crossed the sea
To come here; it is time to return, to go back
1820　To our belovèd lord, Higlac. Denmark
Was a gracious host; you welcomed us
　　　　warmly.
Anything I can do, here on this earth,
To earn your love, oh great king, anything
More than I have done, battles I can fight
1825　In your honor, summon me, I will come as I
　　　　came
Once before. If I hear, from across the ocean,
That your neighbors have threatened you
　　　　with war, or oppressed you
As enemies once oppressed you, here, I will
　　　　bring
A thousand warriors, a thousand armed
　　　　Geats
1830　To protect your throne. I trust Higlac:

Our king is young, but if I need his help
To better help you, to lend you our strength,
Our battle-sharp spears, to shield you and
    honor you
As you deserve, I know his words and his
    deeds
1835 Will support me. And someday, if your oldest
    son,
Hrethric, comes visiting our court, he will find
A host of good friends among the Geats:
No one who goes visiting far-off lands
Is more welcome than a strong and noble
    warrior."
1840   Hrothgar replied:
                    "All-knowing God
Must have sent you such words; nothing so
    wise
From a warrior so young has ever reached
These ancient ears. Your hands are strong,
1845 Your heart and your lips are knowing! If your
    lord,
Hrethel's son, is slain by a spear,
Or falls sick and dies, or is killed by a sword,
And you have survived whatever battle
Sweeps him off, I say that the Geats
1850 Could do no better, find no man better
Suited to be king, keeper of warriors
And their treasure, than you—if you take the
    throne
They will surely offer you. Belovèd Beowulf,
You please me more the longer I can keep you
1855 Here in Denmark. You've turned Danes
And Geats into brothers, brought peace where
    once
There was war, and sealed friendship with
    affection.

This will last as long as I live, and am king
    here:
We will share our treasures, greeting travelers
1860 From across the sea with outstretched hands;
Ring-prowed ships will carry our gifts
And the tokens of our love. Your people live
By the old ways, their hearts, like ours, are
    forever
Open to their friends, but firmly closed
1865 Against their enemies."
                          Then he gave the Geats'
Prince a dozen new gifts, prayed
For his safety, commanded him to seek his
    people,
Yet not to delay too long in visiting
1870 Hrothgar once more. The old king kissed him,
Held that best of all warriors by the shoulder
And wept, unable to hold back his tears.
Gray and wise, he knew how slim
Were his chances of ever greeting Beowulf
1875 Again, but seeing his face he was forced
To hope. His love was too warm to be hidden,
His tears came running too quickly to be
    checked;
His very blood burned with longing.
And then Beowulf left him, left Herot, walked
1880 Across the green in his golden armor,
Exulting in the treasures heaped high in his
    arms.
His ship was at anchor; he had it ready to sail.
And so Hrothgar's rich treasures would leave
    him, travel
Far from that perfect king, without fault
1885 Or blame until winter had followed winter
And age had stolen his strength, spirited it
Off, as it steals from many men.

27

Then the band of Geats, young and brave,
Marching in their ring-locked armor, reached
1890   The shore. The coast-guard saw them coming
And about to go, as he'd seen them before;
He hurried down the hillside, whipping
His horse, but this time shouted no challenge,
Told them only how the Geats would be
     watching
1895   Too, and would welcome such warriors in
     shining
Mail. Their broad-beamed ship lay bobbing
At the edge of the sand: they loaded it high
With armor and horses and all the rich
     treasure
It could hold. The mast stood high and
     straight
1900   Over heaped-up wealth—Hrothgar's, and now
     theirs.
Beowulf rewarded the boat's watchman,
Who had stayed behind, with a sword that
     had hammered
Gold wound on its handle: the weapon
Brought him honor. Then the ship left shore,
     left Denmark,
1905   Traveled through deep water. Deck timbers
     creaked,
And the wind billowing through the sail
     stretched
From the mast, tied tight with ropes, did not
     hold them
Back, did not keep the ring-prowed ship
From foaming swiftly through the waves, the
     sea

1910 Currents, across the wide ocean until
They could see familiar headlands, cliffs
That sprang out of Geatish soil. Driven
By the wind the ship rammed high on the
  shore.
Harbor guards came running to greet them,
1915 Men who for days had waited and watched
For their belovèd comrades to come crossing
  the waves;
They anchored the high-bowed ship, moored it
Close to the shore, where the booming sea
Could not pull it loose and lead it away.
1920 Then they carried up the golden armor,
The ancient swords, the jewels, brought them
To Higlac's home, their ring-giver's hall
Near the sea, where he lived surrounded
By his followers.
1925   He was a famous king, with a fitting
High hall and a wife, Higd,* young
But wise and knowing beyond her years.
She was Hareth's* daughter, a noble queen
With none of the niggardly ways of women
1930 Like Thrith.* Higd gave the Geats gifts
With open hands. But Thrith was too proud,
An imperious princess with a vicious tongue
And so fierce and wild that her father's
  followers
Averted their eyes as she passed, knowing
1935 That if anyone but their king watched where
  she walked
Her hands would shape a noose to fit
Their necks. She would lie, her father's
  lieutenants
Would write out her warrants, and he who had
  stared
Would end his life on the edge of an ancient

1940 Sword. And how great a sin for a woman,
Whether fair or black, to create fear
And destruction, for a woman, who should
     walk in the ways
Of peace, to kill with pretended insults.
But Hemming's* kinsman tamed her: his hall-
     guests
1945 Told a different story, spread the news
That Thrith had forgotten her gory tricks
Once her wise father had sent her to a
     wedding
With Offa,* married her to that brave young
     soldier,
Sent her across the yellow-green sea
1950 To that gold-adorned champion, a fierce
     fighter
In war or peace. They praised her, now,
For her generous heart, and her goodness, and
     the high
And most noble paths she walked, filled
With adoring love for that leader of warriors,
1955 Her husband; he was a man as brave and
     strong
And good, it is said, as anyone on this earth,
A spear-bold soldier who knew no fear,
Exalted with gifts, victorious in war,
A king who ruled his native land
1960 Wisely and well. Emer* was his son,
Hemming's kinsman, Garmund's* grandson,
A powerful swordsman and his warriors'
     shield.

28

Then Beowulf and his men went walking
along
The shore, down the broad strip of sand.
1965 The world's bright candle shone, hurrying
Up from the south. It was a short journey
From their ship to Higlac's home, to the hall
Where their king, Ongentho's* killer, lived
With his warriors and gave treasures away.
They walked
1970 Quickly. The young king knew
They were back, Beowulf and his handful of
brave
Men, come safely home; he sat,
Now, waiting to see them, to greet
His battle-comrades when they arrived at his
court.
1975 They came. And when Beowulf had bowed
to his lord,
And standing in front of the throne had
solemnly
Spoken loyal words, Higlac
Ordered him to sit at his side—he
Who had survived, sailed home victorious,
next to
1980 His kinsman and king. Mead cups were filled
And Hareth's daughter took them through
the hall,
Carried ale to her husband's comrades.
Higlac, unable to stay silent, anxious
To know how Beowulf's adventure had gone,
1985 Began to question him, courteous but eager
To be told everything.
"Belovèd Beowulf,

Tell us what your trip to far-off places
Brought you, your sudden expedition on the
    salty
1990 Waves, your search for war in Herot?
Did you end Hrothgar's hopeless misery,
Could you help that glorious king? Grendel's
Savagery lay heavy on my heart but I was
    afraid
To let you go to him; for a long time
1995 I held you here, kept you safe,
Forced you to make the Danes fight
Their own battles. God be praised
That my eyes have beheld you once more,
    unharmed!"
    Beowulf spoke, Edgetho's brave son:
2000   "My lord Higlac, my meeting with Grendel
And the nighttime battle we fought are known
To everyone in Denmark, where the monster
    was once
The uncrowned ruler, murdering and eating
Hrothgar's people, forever bringing them
2005 Misery. I ended his reign, avenged
His crimes so completely in the crashing
    darkness
That not even the oldest of his evil kind
Will ever boast, lying in sin
And deceit, that the monster beat me. I sought
    out
2010 Hrothgar, first, came to him in his hall;
When Healfdane's famous son heard
That I'd come to challenge Grendel, he gave me
A seat of honor alongside his son.
His followers were drinking; I joined their
    feast,
2015 Sat with that band, as bright and loud-tongued
As any I've ever seen. His famous

Queen went back and forth, hurrying
The cup-bearing boys, giving bracelets
And rings to her husband's warriors. I heard
2020 The oldest soldiers of all calling
For ale from Hrothgar's daughter's hands,
And Freaw* was the way they greeted her
    when she gave them
The golden cups. And Hrothgar will give her
To Ingeld,* gracious Froda's* son;
2025 She and that ripening soldier will be married,
The Danes' great lord and protector has
    declared,
Hoping that his quarrel with the
    Hathobards* can be settled
By a woman. He's wrong: how many wars
Have been put to rest in a prince's bed?
2030 Few. A bride can bring a little
Peace, make spears silent for a time,
But not long. Ingeld and all his men
Will be drinking in the hall, when the
    wedding is done
And Freaw is his wife; the Danes will be
    wearing
2035 Gleaming armor and ring-marked old
    swords;
And the prince and his people will remember
    those treasures,
Will remember that their fathers once wore
    them, fell
With those helmets on their heads, those
    swords in their hands.

29

"And seeing their ancestral armor and
    weapons
2040 Ingeld and his followers will be angry. And
    one
Of his soldiers, sitting with ale in his cup
And bitterness heavy in his heart, will
    remember
War and death, and while he sits and drinks
His sharp old tongue will begin to tempt
2045 Some younger warrior, pushing and probing
For a new war:
               "'That sword, that precious
    old blade
Over there, I think you know it, friend.
Your father carried it, fought with it the last
    time
2050 He could swing a sword; the Danes killed
    him
—And many more of our men—and stripped
The dead bodies: the brave, bold Danes!
One of the princess' people, here,
Now, might be the murderer's son,
2055 Boasting about his treasures, his ancient
Armor—which ought to be yours, by right.'
    "Bitter words will work in a hot-tempered
Brain, pushing up thoughts of the past,
And then, when he can, calling his father's
2060 Name, the youngster will kill some innocent
Dane, a servant—and bloody sword
In hand will run from the hall, knowing
His way through the woods. But war will
    begin
As he runs, to the sound of broken oaths,

2065 And its heat will dry up Ingeld's heart,
Leave him indifferent to his Danish bride.
Hrothgar may think the Hathobards love him,
Loving Freaw, but the friendship can't last,
The vows are worthless.

2070   "But of Grendel: you
                    need to
Know more to know everything; I ought to
Go on. It was early in the evening, Heaven's
Jewel had slid to its rest, and the jealous
Monster, planning murder, came seeking us
2075 Out, stalking us as we guarded Hrothgar's
Hall. Hondshew,* sleeping in his armor,
Was the first Geat he reached: Grendel
Seized him, tore him apart, swallowed him
Down, feet and all, as fate
2080 Had decreed—a glorious young soldier, killed
In his prime. Yet Grendel had only begun
His bloody work, meant to leave us
With his belly and his pouch both full, and
                    Herot
Half-empty. Then he tested his strength
                    against mine,
2085 Hand to hand. His pouch hung
At his side, a huge bag sewn
From a dragon's skin, worked with a devil's
Skill; it was closed by a marvelous clasp.
The monster intended to take me, put me
2090 Inside, save me for another meal.
He was bold and strong, but once I stood
On my feet his strength was useless, and it
                    failed him.

30

"The whole tale of how I killed him,
Repaid him in kind for all the evil
2095 He'd done, would take too long: your people,
My prince, were honored in the doing. He
escaped,
Found a few minutes of life, but his hand,
His whole right arm, stayed in Herot;
The miserable creature crept away,
2100 Dropped to the bottom of his lake, half dead
As he fell. When the sun had returned, the
Danes'
Great king poured out treasure, repaid me
In hammered gold for the bloody battle
I'd fought in his name. He ordered a feast;
2105 There were songs, and the telling of tales. One
ancient
Dane told of long-dead times,
And sometimes Hrothgar himself, with the
harp
In his lap, stroked its silvery strings
And told wonderful stories, a brave king
2110 Reciting unhappy truths about good
And evil—and sometimes he wove his stories
On the mournful thread of old age,
remembering
Buried strength and the battles it had won.
He would weep, the old king, wise with many
2115 Winters, remembering what he'd done, once,
What he'd seen, what he knew. And so we sat
The day away, feasting. Then darkness
Fell again, and Grendel's mother
Was waiting, ready for revenge, hating
2120 The Danes for her son's death. The monstrous

Hag succeeded, burst boldly into Herot
And killed Esher, one of the king's oldest
And wisest soldiers. But when the sun shone
Once more the death-weary Danes could not
    build

2125 A pyre and burn his belovèd body,
Lay him on flaming logs, return ashes
To dust: she'd carried away his corpse,
Brought it to her den deep in the water.
Hrothgar had wept for many of his men,

2130 But this time his heart melted, this
Was the worst. He begged me, in your name,
    half-weeping
As he spoke, to seek still greater glory
Deep in the swirling waves, to win
Still higher fame, and the gifts he would give
    me.

2135 Down in that surging lake I sought
And found her, the horrible hag, fierce
And wild; we fought, clutching and grasping;
The water ran red with blood and at last,
With a mighty sword that had hung on the
    wall,

2140 I cut off her head. I had barely escaped
With my life, my death was not written. And
    the Danes'
Protector, Healfdane's great son, heaped up
Treasures and precious jewels to reward me.

31

"He lived his life as a good king must:

2145 I lost nothing, none of the gifts

My strength could have earned me. He opened
 his store

Of gems and armor, let me choose as I liked,

So I could bring his riches to you, my ruler,

And prove his friendship, and my love. Your
 favor

2150 Still governs my life: I have almost no family,

Higlac, almost no one, now, but you."

 Then Beowulf ordered them to bring in the
 boarhead

Banner, the towering helmet, the ancient,

Silvery armor, and the gold-carved sword:

2155 "This war-gear was Hrothgar's reward, my
 gift

From his wise old hands. He wanted me to tell
 you,

First, whose treasures these were. Hergar

Had owned them, his older brother, who was
 king

Of Denmark until death gave Hrothgar the
 throne:

2160 But Hergar kept them, would not give them to
 Herward,*

His brave young son, though the boy had
 proved

His loyalty. These are yours: may they serve
 you well!"

 And after the gleaming armor four horses

Were led in, four bays, swift and all

2165 Alike. Beowulf had brought his king

Horses and treasure—as a man must,

Not weaving nets of malice for his comrades,
Preparing their death in the dark, with secret,
Cunning tricks. Higlac trusted
2170 His nephew, leaned on his strength, in war,
Each of them intent on the other's joy.
And Beowulf gave Welthow's gift, her
    wonderful
Necklace, to Higd, Higlac's queen,
And gave her, also, three supple, graceful,
2175 Saddle-bright horses; she received his presents,
Then wore that wonderful jewel on her breast.
   So Edgetho's son proved himself,
Did as a famous soldier must do
If glory is what he seeks: not killing his
    comrades
2180 In drunken rages, his heart not savage,
But guarding God's gracious gift, his strength,
Using it only in war, and then using it
Bravely. And yet as a boy he was scorned;
The Geats considered him worthless. When he
    sat
2185 In their mead-hall, and their lord was making
    men rich,
He held no claim on the king's good will.
They were sure he was lazy, noble but slow.
The world spun round, he was a warrior more
    famous
Than any, and all the insults were wiped out.
2190   Then Higlac, protector of his people,
    brought in
His father's—Beowulf's grandfather's—great
    sword,
Worked in gold; none of the Geats
Could boast of a better weapon. He laid it
In Beowulf's lap, then gave him seven
2195 Thousand hides of land, houses

And ground and all. Geatland was home
For both king and prince; their fathers had left
    them
Buildings and fields—but Higlac's inheritance
Stretched further, it was he who was king, and
    was followed.

2200 Afterwards, in the time when Higlac was dead
And Herdred,* his son, who'd ruled the Geats
After his father, had followed him into
    darkness—
Killed in battle with the Swedes, who smashed
His shield, cut through the soldiers
    surrounding
2205 Their king—then, when Higd's one son
Was gone, Beowulf ruled in Geatland,
Took the throne he'd refused, once,
And held it long and well. He was old
With years and wisdom, fifty winters
2210 A king, when a dragon awoke from its
    darkness
And dreams and brought terror to his people.
    The beast
Had slept in a huge stone tower, with a hidden
Path beneath; a man stumbled on
The entrance, went in, discovered the ancient
2215 Treasure, the pagan jewels and gold
The dragon had been guarding, and dazzled
    and greedy
Stole a gem-studded cup, and fled.
But now the dragon hid nothing, neither
The theft nor itself; it swept through the
    darkness,
2220 And all Geatland knew its anger.

32

But the thief had not come to steal; he stole,
And roused the dragon, not from desire
But need. He was someone's slave, had been
  beaten
By his masters, had run from all men's sight,
2225 But with no place to hide; then he found the
  hidden
Path, and used it. And once inside,
Seeing the sleeping beast, staring as it
Yawned and stretched, not wanting to wake it,
Terror-struck, he turned and ran for his life,
2230 Taking the jeweled cup.
                              That tower
Was heaped high with hidden treasure, stored
  there
Years before by the last survivor
Of a noble race, ancient riches
2235 Left in the darkness as the end of a dynasty
Came. Death had taken them, one
By one, and the warrior who watched over all
That remained mourned their fate, expecting,
Soon, the same for himself, knowing
2240 The gold and jewels he had guarded so long
Could not bring him pleasure much longer. He
  brought
The precious cups, the armor and the ancient
Swords, to a stone tower built
Near the sea, below a cliff, a sealed
2245 Fortress with no windows, no doors, waves
In front of it, rocks behind. Then he spoke:
    "Take these treasures, earth, now that no
      one

Living can enjoy them. They were yours, in the
    beginning;
Allow them to return. War and terror
2250 Have swept away my people, shut
Their eyes to delight and to living, closed
The door to all gladness. No one is left
To lift these swords, polish these jeweled
Cups: no one leads, no one follows. These
    hammered
2255 Helmets, worked with gold, will tarnish
And crack; the hands that should clean and
    polish them
Are still forever. And these mail shirts, worn
In battle, once, while swords crashed
And blades bit into shields and men,
2260 Will rust away like the warriors who owned
    them.
None of these treasures will travel to distant
Lands, following their lords. The harp's
Bright song, the hawk crossing through the
    hall
On its swift wings, the stallion tramping
2265 In the courtyard—all gone, creatures of every
Kind, and their masters, hurled to the grave!"
    And so he spoke, sadly, of those
Long dead, and lived from day to day,
Joyless, until, at last, death touched
2270 His heart and took him too. And a stalker
In the night, a flaming dragon, found
The treasure unguarded; he whom men fear
Came flying through the darkness, wrapped in
    fire,
Seeking caves and stone-split ruins
2275 But finding gold. Then it stayed, buried
Itself with heathen silver and jewels

It could neither use nor ever abandon.
     So mankind's enemy, the mighty beast,
Slept in those stone walls for hundreds
2280 Of years; a runaway slave roused it,
Stole a jeweled cup and bought
His master's forgiveness, begged for mercy
And was pardoned when his delighted lord
     took the present
He bore, turned it in his hands and stared
2285 At the ancient carvings. The cup brought
     peace
To a slave, pleased his master, but stirred
A dragon's anger. It turned, hunting
The thief's tracks, and found them, saw
Where its visitor had come and gone. He'd
     survived,
2290 Had come close enough to touch its scaly
Head and yet lived, as it lifted its cavernous
Jaws, through the grace of almighty God
And a pair of quiet, quick-moving feet.
The dragon followed his steps, anxious
2295 To find the man who had robbed it of silver
And sleep; it circled around and around
The tower, determined to catch him, but
     could not,
He had run too fast, the wilderness was
     empty.
The beast went back to its treasure, planning
2300 A bloody revenge, and found what was
     missing,
Saw what thieving hands had stolen.
Then it crouched on the stones, counting off
The hours till the Almighty's candle went out,
And evening came, and wild with anger
2305 It could fly burning across the land, killing

And destroying with its breath. Then the sun
    was gone,
And its heart was glad: glowing with rage
It left the tower, impatient to repay
Its enemies. The people suffered, everyone
2310 Lived in terror, but when Beowulf had
    learned
Of their trouble his fate was worse, and came
    quickly.

33

Vomiting fire and smoke, the dragon
Burned down their homes. They watched in
    horror
As the flames rose up: the angry monster
2315 Meant to leave nothing alive. And the signs
Of its anger flickered and glowed in the
    darkness,
Visible for miles, tokens of its hate
And its cruelty, spread like a warning to the
    Geats
Who had broken its rest. Then it hurried back
2320 To its tower, to its hidden treasure, before
    dawn
Could come. It had wrapped its flames around
The Geats; now it trusted in stone
Walls, and its strength, to protect it. But they
    would not.
    Then they came to Beowulf, their king, and
    announced
2325 That his hall, his throne, the best of buildings,

Had melted away in the dragon's burning
Breath. Their words brought misery,
        Beowulf's
Sorrow beat at his heart: he accused
Himself of breaking God's law, of bringing
2330   The Almighty's anger down on his people.
Reproach pounded in his breast, gloomy
And dark, and the world seemed a different
        place.
But the hall was gone, the dragon's molten
Breath had licked across it, burned it
2335   To ashes, near the shore it had guarded. The
        Geats
Deserved revenge; Beowulf, their leader
And lord, began to plan it, ordered
A battle-shield shaped of iron, knowing that
Wood would be useless, that no linden shield
2340   Could help him, protect him, in the flaming
        heat
Of the beast's breath. That noble prince
Would end his days on earth, soon,
Would leave this brief life, but would take
        the dragon
With him, tear it from the heaped-up treasure
2345   It had guarded so long. And he'd go to it
        alone,
Scorning to lead soldiers against such
An enemy: he saw nothing to fear, thought
        nothing
Of the beast's claws, or wings, or flaming
Jaws—he had fought, before, against worse
2350   Odds, had survived, been victorious, in
        harsher
Battles, beginning in Herot, Hrothgar's
Unlucky hall. He'd killed Grendel
And his mother, swept that murdering tribe

Away. And he'd fought in Higlac's war
2355 With the Frisians, fought at his lord's side
Till a sword reached out and drank Higlac's
Blood, till a blade swung in the rush
Of battle killed the Geats' great king.
Then Beowulf escaped, broke through Frisian
2360 Shields and swam to freedom, saving
Thirty sets of armor from the scavenging
Franks, river people who robbed
The dead as they floated by. Beowulf
Offered them only his sword, ended
2365 So many jackal lives that the few
Who were able skulked silently home, glad
To leave him. So Beowulf swam sadly back
To Geatland, almost the only survivor
Of a foolish war. Higlac's widow
2370 Brought him the crown, offered him the
        kingdom,
Not trusting Herdred, her son and Higlac's,
To beat off foreign invaders. But Beowulf
Refused to rule when his lord's own son
Was alive, and the leaderless Geats could
        choose
2375 A rightful king. He gave Herdred
All his support, offering an open
Heart where Higlac's young son could see
Wisdom he still lacked himself: warmth
And good will were what Beowulf brought
        his new king.
2380   But Swedish exiles came, seeking
Protection; they were rebels against Onela,
Healfdane's son-in-law and the best ring-giver
His people had ever known. And Onela
Came too, a mighty king, marched
2385 On Geatland with a huge army; Herdred
Had given his word and now he gave

His life, shielding the Swedish strangers
Onela wanted nothing more:
When Herdred had fallen that famous warrior
2390 Went back to Sweden, let Beowulf rule!

34

But Beowulf remembered how his king had
   been killed.
As soon as he could he lent the last
Of the Swedish rebels soldiers and gold,
Helped him to a bitter battle across
2395 The wide sea, where victory, and revenge, and
   the Swedish
Throne were won, and Onela was slain.
   So Edgetho's son survived, no matter
What dangers he met, what battles he fought,
Brave and forever triumphant, till the day
2400 Fate sent him to the dragon and sent him
   death.
A dozen warriors walked with their angry
King, when he was brought to the beast;
   Beowulf
Knew, by then, what had woken the monster,
And enraged it. The cup had come to him,
   traveled
2405 From dragon to slave, to master, to king,
And the slave was their guide, had begun the
   Geats'
Affliction, and now, afraid of both beast
And men, was forced to lead them to the
   monster's
Hidden home. He showed them the huge

2410 Stones, set deep in the ground, with the sea
Beating on the rocks close by. Beowulf
Stared, listening to stories of the gold
And riches heaped inside. Hidden,
But wakeful, now, the dragon waited,
2415 Ready to greet him. Gold and hammered
Armor have been buried in pleasanter places!
The battle-brave king rested on the shore,
While his soldiers wished him well, urged him
On. But Beowulf's heart was heavy:
2420 His soul sensed how close fate
Had come, felt something, not fear but
knowledge
Of old age. His armor was strong, but his arm
Hung like his heart. Body and soul
Might part, here; his blood might be spilled,
2425 His spirit torn from his flesh. Then he spoke.
"My early days were full of war,
And I survived it all; I can remember
everything.
I was seven years old when Hrethel opened
His home and his heart for me, when my king
and lord
2430 Took me from my father and kept me, taught
me,
Gave me gold and pleasure, glad that I sat
At his knee. And he never loved me less
Than any of his sons—Herbald,* the oldest
Of all, or Hathcyn,* or Higlac, my lord.
2435 Herbald died a horrible death,
Killed while hunting: Hathcyn, his brother,
Stretched his horn-tipped bow, sent
An arrow flying, but missed his mark
And hit Herbald instead, found him
2440 With a bloody point and pierced him through.
The crime was great, the guilt was plain,

But nothing could be done, no vengeance, no
   death
To repay that death, no punishment, nothing.
   "So with the graybeard whose son sins
2445 Against the king, and is hanged: he stands
Watching his child swing on the gallows,
Lamenting, helpless, while his flesh and blood
Hangs for the raven to pluck. He can raise
His voice in sorrow, but revenge is impossible.
2450 And every morning he remembers how his son
Died, and despairs; no son to come
Matters, no future heir, to a father
Forced to live through such misery. The place
Where his son once dwelled, before death
   compelled him
2455 To journey away, is a windy wasteland,
Empty, cheerless; the childless father
Shudders, seeing it. So riders and ridden
Sleep in the ground; pleasure is gone,
The harp is silent, and hope is forgotten.

35

2460   "And then, crying his sorrow, he crawls
To his bed: the world, and his home, hurt him
With their emptiness. And so it seemed to
   Hrethel,
When Herbald was dead, and his heart swelled
With grief. The murderer lived; he felt
2465 No love for him, now, but nothing could help,
Word nor hand nor sharp-honed blade,
War nor hate, battle or blood
Or law. The pain could find no relief,

He could only live with it, or leave grief and
    life
2470 Together. When he'd gone to his grave Hathcyn
And Higlac, his sons, inherited everything.
    "And then there was war between Geats and
    Swedes,
Bitter battles carried across
The broad sea, when the mighty Hrethel slept
2475 And Ongentho's sons thought Sweden could
    safely
Attack, saw no use to pretending friendship
But raided and burned, and near old
    Rennsburg*
Slaughtered Geats with their thieving swords.
My people repaid them, death for death,
2480 Battle for battle, though one of the brothers
Bought that revenge with his life—Hathcyn,
King of the Geats, killed by a Swedish
Sword. But when dawn came the slayer
Was slain, and Higlac's soldiers avenged
2485 Everything with the edge of their blades. Efor*
Caught the Swedish king, cracked
His helmet, split his skull, dropped him,
Pale and bleeding, to the ground, then put him
To death with a swift stroke, shouting
2490 His joy.
    "The gifts that Higlac gave me,
And the land, I earned with my sword, as fate
Allowed: he never needed Danes
Or Goths* or Swedes, soldiers and allies
2495 Bought with gold, bribed to his side.
My sword was better, and always his.
In every battle my place was in front,
Alone, and so it shall be forever,
As long as this sword lasts, serves me
2500 In the future as it has served me before. So

I killed Dagref,* the Frank, who brought death
To Higlac, and who looted his corpse: Higd's
Necklace, Welthow's treasure, never
Came to Dagref's king. The thief
2505 Fell in battle, but not on my blade.
He was brave and strong, but I swept him in
    my arms,
Ground him against me till his bones broke,
Till his blood burst out. And now I shall fight
For this treasure, fight with both hand and
    sword."
2510   And Beowulf uttered his final boast:
    "I've never known fear; as a youth I fought
In endless battles. I am old, now,
But I will fight again, seek fame still,
If the dragon hiding in his tower dares
2515 To face me."
               Then he said farewell to his
    followers,
Each in his turn, for the last time:
    "I'd use no sword, no weapon, if this beast
Could be killed without it, crushed to death
2520 Like Grendel, gripped in my hands and torn
Limb from limb. But his breath will be burning
Hot, poison will pour from his tongue.
I feel no shame, with shield and sword
And armor, against this monster: when he
    comes to me
2525 I mean to stand, not run from his shooting
Flames, stand till fate decides
Which of us wins. My heart is firm,
My hands calm: I need no hot
Words. Wait for me close by, my friends.
2530 We shall see, soon, who will survive
This bloody battle, stand when the fighting
Is done. No one else could do

What I mean to, here, no man but me
Could hope to defeat this monster. No one
2535   Could try. And this dragon's treasure, his
        gold
And everything hidden in that tower, will be
        mine
Or war will sweep me to a bitter death!"
    Then Beowulf rose, still brave, still strong,
And with his shield at his side, and a mail
        shirt on his breast,
2540   Strode calmly, confidently, toward the tower,
        under
The rocky cliffs: no coward could have
        walked there!
And then he who'd endured dozens of
        desperate
Battles, who'd stood boldly while swords and
        shields
Clashed, the best of kings, saw
2545   Huge stone arches and felt the heat
Of the dragon's breath, flooding down
Through the hidden entrance, too hot for
        anyone
To stand, a streaming current of fire
And smoke that blocked all passage. And the
        Geats'
2550   Lord and leader, angry, lowered
His sword and roared out a battle cry,
A call so loud and clear that it reached
        through
The hoary rock, hung in the dragon's
Ear. The beast rose, angry,
2555   Knowing a man had come—and then nothing
But war could have followed. Its breath came
        first,
A steaming cloud pouring from the stone,

Then the earth itself shook. Beowulf
Swung his shield into place, held it
2560 In front of him, facing the entrance. The
    dragon
Coiled and uncoiled, its heart urging it
Into battle. Beowulf's ancient sword
Was waiting, unsheathed, his sharp and
    gleaming
Blade. The beast came closer; both of them
2565 Were ready, each set on slaughter. The Geats'
Great prince stood firm, unmoving, prepared
Behind his high shield, waiting in his shining
Armor. The monster came quickly toward him,
Pouring out fire and smoke, hurrying
2570 To its fate. Flames beat at the iron
Shield, and for a time it held, protected
Beowulf as he'd planned; then it began to melt,
And for the first time in his life that famous
    prince
Fought with fate against him, with glory
2575 Denied him. He knew it, but he raised his
    sword
And struck at the dragon's scaly hide.
The ancient blade broke, bit into
The monster's skin, drew blood, but cracked
And failed him before it went deep enough,
    helped him
2580 Less than he needed. The dragon leaped
With pain, thrashed and beat at him, spouting
Murderous flames, spreading them everywhere.
And the Geats' ring-giver did not boast of
    glorious
Victories in other wars: his weapon
2585 Had failed him, deserted him, now when he
    needed it
Most, that excellent sword. Edgetho's

Famous son stared at death,
Unwilling to leave this world, to exchange it
For a dwelling in some distant place—a
    journey
2590 Into darkness that all men must make, as death
Ends their few brief hours on earth.
    Quickly, the dragon came at him,
        encouraged
As Beowulf fell back; its breath flared,
And he suffered, wrapped around in swirling
2595 Flames—a king, before, but now
A beaten warrior. None of his comrades
Came to him, helped him, his brave and noble
Followers; they ran for their lives, fled
Deep in a wood. And only one of them
2600 Remained, stood there, miserable,
        remembering
As a good man must, what kinship should
        mean.

36

    His name was Wiglaf,* he was Wexstan's*
        son
And a good soldier; his family had been
        Swedish,
Once. Watching Beowulf, he could see
2605 How his king was suffering, burning.
        Remembering
Everything his lord and cousin had given him,
Armor and gold and the great estates
Wexstan's family enjoyed, Wiglaf's
Mind was made up; he raised his yellow

2610   Shield and drew his sword—an ancient
Weapon that had once belonged to Onela's
Nephew, and that Wexstan had won, killing
The prince when he fled from Sweden, sought
      safety
With Herdred, and found death. And Wiglaf's
      father
2615   Had carried the dead man's armor, and his
      sword,
To Onela, and the king had said nothing, only
Given him armor and sword and all,
Everything his rebel nephew had owned
And lost when he left this life. And Wexstan
2620   Had kept those shining gifts, held them
For years, waiting for his son to use them,
Wear them as honorably and well as once
His father had done; then Wexstan died
And Wiglaf was his heir, inherited treasures
2625   And weapons and land. He'd never worn
That armor, fought with that sword, until
      Beowulf
Called him to his side, led him into war.
But his soul did not melt, his sword was
      strong;
The dragon discovered his courage, and his
      weapon,
2630   When the rush of battle brought them
      together.
    And Wiglaf, his heart heavy, uttered
The kind of words his comrades deserved:
    "I remember how we sat in the mead-hall,
      drinking
And boasting of how brave we'd be when
      Beowulf
2635   Needed us, he who gave us these swords
And armor: all of us swore to repay him,

When the time came, kindness for kindness
—With our lives, if he needed them. He
    allowed us to join him,
Chose us from all his great army, thinking
2640 Our boasting words had some weight,
    believing
Our promises, trusting our swords. He took us
For soldiers, for men. He meant to kill
This monster himself, our mighty king,
Fight this battle alone and unaided,
2645 As in the days when his strength and daring
    dazzled
Men's eyes. But those days are over and gone
And now our lord must lean on younger
Arms. And we must go to him, while angry
Flames burn at his flesh, help
2650 Our glorious king! By almighty God,
I'd rather burn myself than see
Flames swirling around my lord.
And who are we to carry home
Our shields before we've slain his enemy
2655 And ours, to run back to our homes with
    Beowulf
So hard-pressed here? I swear that nothing
He ever did deserved an end
Like this, dying miserably and alone,
Butchered by this savage beast: we swore
2660 That these swords and armor were each for us
    all!"
    Then he ran to his king, crying
    encouragement
As he dove through the dragon's deadly fumes:
    "Belovèd Beowulf, remember how you
    boasted,
Once, that nothing in the world would ever
2665 Destroy your fame: fight to keep it,

Now, be strong and brave, my noble
King, protecting life and fame
Together. My sword will fight at your side!"
      The dragon heard him, the man-hating
            monster,
2670 And was angry; shining with surging flames
It came for him, anxious to return his visit.
Waves of fire swept at his shield
And the edge began to burn. His mail shirt
Could not help him, but before his hands
            dropped
2675 The blazing wood Wiglaf jumped
Behind Beowulf's shield; his own was burned
To ashes. Then the famous old hero,
            remembering
Days of glory, lifted what was left
Of Nagling,* his ancient sword, and swung it
2680 With all his strength, smashed the gray
Blade into the beast's head. But then Nagling
Broke to pieces, as iron always
Had in Beowulf's hands. His arms
Were too strong, the hardest blade could not
            help him,
2685 The most wonderfully worked. He carried
      them to war
But fate had decreed that the Geats' great
            king
Would be no better for any weapon.
      Then the monster charged again, vomiting
Fire, wild with pain, rushed out
2690 Fierce and dreadful, its fear forgotten.
Watching for its chance it drove its tusks
Into Beowulf's neck; he staggered, the blood
Came flooding forth, fell like rain.

37

2695
And then when Beowulf needed him most
Wiglaf showed his courage, his strength
And skill, and the boldness he was born with.
    Ignoring
The dragon's head, he helped his lord
By striking lower down. The sword
Sank in; his hand was burned, but the shining

2700
Blade had done its work, the dragon's
Belching flames began to flicker
And die away. And Beowulf drew
His battle-sharp dagger: the blood-stained old king
Still knew what he was doing. Quickly, he cut

2705
The beast in half, slit it apart.
It fell, their courage had killed it, two noble
Cousins had joined in the dragon's death.
Yet what they did all men must do
When the time comes! But the triumph was
    the last

2710
Beowulf would ever earn, the end
Of greatness and life together. The wound
In his neck began to swell and grow;
He could feel something stirring, burning
In his veins, a stinging venom, and knew

2715
The beast's fangs had left it. He fumbled
Along the wall, found a slab
Of stone, and dropped down; above him he
    saw
Huge stone arches and heavy posts,
Holding up the roof of that giant hall.

2720
Then Wiglaf's gentle hands bathed
The blood-stained prince, his glorious lord,
Weary of war, and loosened his helmet.

Beowulf spoke, in spite of the swollen,
Livid wound, knowing he'd unwound
2725 His string of days on earth, seen
As much as God would grant him; all worldly
Pleasure was gone, as life would go,
Soon:

"I'd leave my armor to my son,
2730 Now, if God had given me an heir,
A child born of my body, his life
Created from mine. I've worn this crown
For fifty winters: no neighboring people
Have tried to threaten the Geats, sent soldiers
2735 Against us or talked of terror. My days
Have gone by as fate willed, waiting
For its word to be spoken, ruling as well
As I knew how, swearing no unholy oaths,
Seeking no lying wars. I can leave
2740 This life happy; I can die, here,
Knowing the Lord of all life has never
Watched me wash my sword in blood
Born of my own family. Belovèd
Wiglaf, go, quickly, find
2745 The dragon's treasure: we've taken its life,
But its gold is ours, too. Hurry,
Bring me ancient silver, precious
Jewels, shining armor and gems,
Before I die. Death will be softer,
2750 Leaving life and this people I've ruled
So long, if I look at this last of all prizes."

38

Then Wexstan's son went in, as quickly
As he could, did as the dying Beowulf
Asked, entered the inner darkness
2755   Of the tower, went with his mail shirt and his
            sword.
Flushed with victory he groped his way,
A brave young warrior, and suddenly saw
Piles of gleaming gold, precious
Gems, scattered on the floor, cups
2760   And bracelets, rusty old helmets, beautifully
Made but rotting with no hands to rub
And polish them. They lay where the dragon
            left them;
It had flown in the darkness, once, before
            fighting
Its final battle. (So gold can easily
2765   Triumph, defeat the strongest of men,
No matter how deep it is hidden!) And he
            saw,
Hanging high above, a golden
Banner, woven by the best of weavers
And beautiful. And over everything he saw
2770   A strange light, shining everywhere,
On walls and floor and treasure. Nothing
Moved, no other monsters appeared;
He took what he wanted, all the treasures
That pleased his eye, heavy plates
2775   And golden cups and the glorious banner,
Loaded his arms with all they could hold.
Beowulf's dagger, his iron blade,
Had finished the fire-spitting terror
That once protected tower and treasures
2780   Alike; the gray-bearded lord of the Geats

Had ended those flying, burning raids
Forever.
                    Then Wiglaf went back, anxious
To return while Beowulf was alive, to bring
        him
2785   Treasure they'd won together. He ran,
Hoping his wounded king, weak
And dying, had not left the world too soon.
Then he brought their treasure to Beowulf,
        and found
His famous king bloody, gasping
2790   For breath. But Wiglaf sprinkled water
Over his lord, until the words
Deep in his breast broke through and were
        heard.
Beholding the treasure he spoke, haltingly:
    "For this, this gold, these jewels, I thank
2795   Our Father in Heaven, Ruler of the Earth—
For all of this, that His grace has given me,
Allowed me to bring to my people while
        breath
Still came to my lips. I sold my life
For this treasure, and I sold it well. Take
2800   What I leave, Wiglaf, lead my people,
Help them; my time is gone. Have
The brave Geats build me a tomb,
When the funeral flames have burned me, and
        build it
Here, at the water's edge, high
2805   On this spit of land, so sailors can see
This tower, and remember my name, and call it
Beowulf's tower, and boats in the darkness
And mist, crossing the sea, will know it."
            Then that brave king gave the golden
2810   Necklace from around his throat to Wiglaf,

Gave him his gold-covered helmet, and his
　　rings,
And his mail shirt, and ordered him to use
　　them well:
　　"You're the last of all our far-flung family.
Fate has swept our race away,
2815　Taken warriors in their strength and led them
To the death that was waiting. And now I
　　follow them."
　　The old man's mouth was silent, spoke
No more, had said as much as it could;
He would sleep in the fire, soon. His soul
2820　Left his flesh, flew to glory.

39

　　And then Wiglaf was left, a young warrior
Sadly watching his belovèd king,
Seeing him stretched on the ground, left
　　guarding
A torn and bloody corpse. But Beowulf's
2825　Killer was dead, too, the coiled
Dragon, cut in half, cold
And motionless: men, and their swords, had
　　swept it
From the earth, left it lying in front of
Its tower, won its treasure when it fell
2830　Crashing to the ground, cut it apart
With their hammered blades, driven them
　　deep in
Its belly. It would never fly through the night,
Glowing in the dark sky, glorying

In its riches, burning and raiding: two
    warriors
2835 Had shown it their strength, slain it with
    their swords.
Not many men, no matter how strong,
No matter how daring, how bold, had done
As well, rushing at its venomous fangs,
Or even quietly entering its tower,
2840 Intending to steal but finding the treasure's
Guardian awake, watching and ready
To greet them. Beowulf had gotten its gold,
Bought it with blood; dragon and king
Had ended each other's days on earth.
2845   And when the battle was over Beowulf's
    followers
Came out of the wood, cowards and traitors,
Knowing the dragon was dead. Afraid,
While it spit its fires, to fight in their lord's
Defense, to throw their javelins and spears,
2850 They came like shamefaced jackals, their
    shields
In their hands, to the place where the prince
    lay dead,
And waited for Wiglaf to speak. He was
    sitting
Near Beowulf's body, wearily sprinkling
Water in the dead man's face, trying
2855 To stir him. He could not. No one could
    have kept
Life in their lord's body, or turned
Aside the Lord's will: world
And men and all move as He orders,
And always have, and always will.
2860   Then Wiglaf turned and angrily told them
What men without courage must hear.
Wexstan's brave son stared at the traitors,

His heart sorrowful, and said what he had
    to:
    "I say what anyone who speaks the truth
2865 Must say. Your lord gave you gifts,
Swords and the armor you stand in now;
You sat on the mead-hall benches, prince
And followers, and he gave you, with open
    hands,
Helmets and mail shirts, hunted across
2870 The world for the best of weapons. War
Came and you ran like cowards, dropped
Your swords as soon as the danger was real.
Should Beowulf have boasted of your help,
    rejoiced
In your loyal strength? With God's good
    grace
2875 He helped himself, swung his sword
Alone, won his own revenge.
The help I gave him was nothing, but all
I was able to give; I went to him, knowing
That nothing but Beowulf's strength could
    save us,
2880 And my sword was lucky, found some vital
Place and bled the burning flames
Away. Too few of his warriors remembered
To come, when our lord faced death, alone.
And now the giving of swords, of golden
2885 Rings and rich estates, is over,
Ended for you and everyone who shares
Your blood: when the brave Geats hear
How you bolted and ran none of your race
Will have anything left but their lives. And
    death
2890 Would be better for them all, and for you,
    than the kind
Of life you can lead, branded with disgrace!"

40

Then Wiglaf ordered a messenger to ride
Across the cliff, to the Geats who'd waited
The morning away, sadly wondering
2895   If their belovèd king would return, or be
        killed,
A troop of soldiers sitting in silence
And hoping for the best. Whipping his horse
The herald came to them; they crowded
        around,
And he told them everything, present and
        past:
2900   "Our lord is dead, leader of this people.
The dragon killed him, but the beast is dead,
Too, cut in half by a dagger;
Beowulf's enemy sleeps in its blood.
No sword could pierce its skin, wound
2905   That monster. Wiglaf is sitting in mourning,
Close to Beowulf's body, Wexstan's
Weary son, silent and sad,
Keeping watch for our king, there
Where Beowulf and the beast that killed him
        lie dead.
2910   "And this people can expect fighting, once
The Franks, and the Frisians, have heard that
        our king
Lies dead. The news will spread quickly.
Higlac began our bitter quarrel
With the Franks, raiding along their river
2915   Rhine with ships and soldiers, until
They attacked him with a huge army, and
        Higlac
Was killed, the king and many of our men,
Mailed warriors defeated in war,

Beaten by numbers. He brought no treasure
2920 To the mead-hall, after that battle. And ever
After we knew no friendship with the Franks.
    "Nor can we expect peace from the
        Swedes.
Everyone knows how their old king,
Ongentho, killed Hathcyn, caught him
2925 Near a wood when our young lord went
To war too soon, dared too much.
The wise old Swede, always terrible
In war, allowed the Geats to land
And begin to loot, then broke them with a
        lightning
2930 Attack, taking back treasure and his
        kidnaped
Queen, and taking our king's life.
And then he followed his beaten enemies,
Drove them in front of Swedish swords
Until darkness dropped, and weary, lordless,
2935 They could hide in the wood. But he waited,
        Ongentho
With his mass of soldiers, circled around
The Geats who'd survived, who'd escaped
        him, calling
Threats and boasts at that wretched band
The whole night through. In the morning
        he'd hang
2940 A few, he promised, to amuse the birds,
Then slaughter the rest. But the sun rose
To the sound of Higlac's horns and trumpets,
Light and that battle cry coming together
And turning sadhearted Geats into soldiers.
2945 Higlac had followed his people, and found
        them.

41

"Then blood was everywhere, two bands of
    Geats
Falling on the Swedes, men fighting
On all sides, butchering each other.
Sadly, Ongentho ordered his soldiers
2950 Back, to the high ground where he'd built
A fortress; he'd heard of Higlac, knew
His boldness and strength. Out in the open
He could never resist such a soldier, defend
Hard-won treasure, Swedish wives
2955 And children, against the Geats' new king.
Brave but wise, he fled, sought safety
Behind earthen walls. Eagerly, the Geats
Followed, sweeping across the field,
Smashing through the walls, waving Higlac's
2960 Banners as they came. Then the gray-haired old
    king
Was brought to bay, bright sword-blades
Forcing the lord of the Swedes to take
Judgment at Efor's hands. Efor's
Brother, Wulf, raised his weapon
2965 First, swung it angrily at the fierce
Old king, cracked his helmet; blood
Seeped through his hair. But the brave old
    Swede
Felt no fear: he quickly returned
A better blow than he'd gotten, faced
2970 Toward Wulf* and struck him savagely. And
    Efor's
Bold brother was staggered, half raised his
    sword
But only dropped it to the ground. Ongentho's

Blade had cut through his helmet, his head
Spouted blood, and slowly he fell.
2975 The wound was deep, but death was not due
So soon; fate let him recover, live
On. But Efor, his brave brother,
Seeing Wulf fall, came forward with his
    broadbladed
Sword, hammered by giants, and swung it
2980 So hard that Ongentho's shield shattered
And he sank to the earth, his life ended.
Then, with the battlefield theirs, the Geats
Rushed to Wulf's side, raised him up
And bound his wound. Wulf's brother
2985 Stripped the old Swede, took
His iron mail shirt, his hilted sword
And his helmet, and all his ancient war-gear,
And brought them to Higlac, his new lord.
The king welcomed him, warmly thanked
    him
2990 For his gifts and promised, there where
    everyone
Could hear, that as soon as he sat in his
    mead-hall
Again Efor and Wulf would have treasure
Heaped in their battle-hard hands; he'd repay
    them
Their bravery with wealth, give them gold
2995 And lands and silver rings, rich rewards for
    the glorious
Deeds they'd done with their swords. The
    Geats agreed. And to prove
Efor's grace in his eyes, Higlac
Swore he'd give him his only daughter.
    "These are the quarrels, the hatreds, the
        feuds,

3000 That will bring us battles, force us into war
With the Swedes, as soon as they've learned
        how our lord
Is dead, know that the Geats are leaderless,
Have lost the best of kings, Beowulf—
He who held our enemies away,
3005 Kept land and treasure intact, who saved
Hrothgar and the Danes—he who lived
All his long life bravely. Then let us
Go to him, hurry to our glorious lord,
Behold him lifeless, and quickly carry him
3010 To the flames. The fire must melt more
Than his bones, more than his share of
        treasure:
Give it all of this golden pile,
This terrible, uncounted heap of cups
And rings, bought with his blood. Burn it
3015 To ashes, to nothingness. No one living
Should enjoy these jewels; no beautiful
        women
Wear them, gleaming and golden, from their
        necks,
But walk, instead, sad and alone
In a hundred foreign lands, their laughter
3020 Gone forever, as Beowulf's has gone,
His pleasure and his joy. Spears shall be
        lifted,
Many cold mornings, lifted and thrown,
And warriors shall waken to no harp's bright
        call
But the croak of the dark-black raven, ready
3025 To welcome the dead, anxious to tell
The eagle how he stuffed his craw with
        corpses,
Filled his belly even faster than the wolves."
        And so the messenger spoke, a brave

Man on an ugly errand, telling
3030 Only the truth. Then the warriors rose,
Walked slowly down from the cliff, stared
At those wonderful sights, stood weeping as
they saw
Beowulf dead on the sand, their bold
Ring-giver resting in his last bed;
3035 He'd reached the end of his days, their
mighty
War-king, the great lord of the Geats,
Gone to a glorious death. But they saw
The dragon first, stretched in front
Of its tower, a strange, scaly beast
3040 Gleaming a dozen colors dulled and
Scorched in its own heat. From end
To end fifty feet, it had flown
In the silent darkness, a swift traveler
Tasting the air, then gliding down
3045 To its den. Death held it in his hands;
It would guard no caves, no towers, keep
No treasures like the cups, the precious plates
Spread where it lay, silver and brass
Encrusted and rotting, eaten away
3050 As though buried in the earth for a thousand
winters.
And all this ancient hoard, huge
And golden, was wound around with a spell:
No man could enter the tower, open
Hidden doors, unless the Lord
3055 Of Victories, He who watches over men,
Almighty God Himself, was moved
To let him enter, and him alone.

42

Hiding that treasure deep in its tower,
As the dragon had done, broke God's law
3060 And brought it no good. Guarding its stolen
Wealth it killed Wiglaf's king,
But was punished with death. Who knows when princes
And their soldiers, the bravest and strongest of men,
Are destined to die, their time ended,
3065 Their homes, their halls empty and still?
So Beowulf sought out the dragon, dared it
Into battle, but could never know what God
Had decreed, or that death would come to him, or why.
So the spell was solemnly laid, by men
3070 Long dead; it was meant to last till the day
Of judgment. Whoever stole their jewels,
Their gold, would be cursed with the flames of hell,
Heaped high with sin and guilt, if greed
Was what brought him: God alone could break
3075 Their magic, open His grace to man.
      Then Wiglaf spoke, Wexstan's son:
      "How often an entire country suffers
On one man's account! That time has come to us:
We tried to counsel our belovèd king,
3080 Our shield and protection, show him danger,
Urge him to leave the dragon in the dark
Tower it had lain in so long, live there
Till the end of the world. Fate, and his will,
Were too strong. Everyone knows the treasure
3085 His life bought: but Beowulf was worth

More than this gold, and the gift is a harsh
    one.
I've seen it all, been in the tower
Where the jewels and armor were hidden,
    allowed
To behold them once war and its terror were
    done.
3090 I gathered them up, gold and silver,
Filled my arms as full as I could
And quickly carried them back to my king.
He lay right here, still alive,
Still sure in mind and tongue. He spoke
3095 Sadly, said I should greet you, asked
That after you'd burned his body you bring
His ashes here, make this the tallest
Of towers and his tomb—as great and lasting
As his fame, when Beowulf himself walked
3100 The earth and no man living could match
    him.
Come, let us enter the tower, see
The dragon's marvelous treasure one
Last time: I'll lead the way, take you
Close to that heap of curious jewels,
3105 And rings, and gold. Let the pyre be ready
And high: as soon as we've seen the dragon's
Hoard we will carry our belovèd king,
Our leader and lord, where he'll lie forever
In God's keeping."
3110   Then Wiglaf commanded
The wealthiest Geats, brave warriors
And owners of land, leaders of his people,
To bring wood for Beowulf's funeral:
    "Now the fire must feed on his body,
3115 Flames grow heavy and black with him
Who endured arrows falling in iron
Showers, feathered shafts, barbed

And sharp, shot through linden shields,
Storms of eager arrowheads dropping."

3120   And Wextan's wise son took seven
Of the noblest Geats, led them together
Down the tunnel, deep into the dragon's
Tower; the one in front had a torch,
Held it high in his hands. The best
3125   Of Beowulf's followers entered behind
That gleaming flame: seeing gold
And silver rotting on the ground, with no
        one
To guard it, the Geats were not troubled with
        scruples
Or fears, but quickly gathered up
3130   Treasure and carried it out of the tower.
And they rolled the dragon down to the cliff
And dropped it over, let the ocean take it,
The tide sweep it away. Then silver
And gold and precious jewels were put
3135   On a wagon, with Beowulf's body, and
        brought
Down the jutting sand, where the pyre
        waited.

43

A huge heap of wood was ready,
Hung around with helmets, and battle
Shields, and shining mail shirts, all
3140   As Beowulf had asked. The bearers brought
Their belovèd lord, their glorious king,
And weeping laid him high on the wood.

Then the warriors began to kindle that
    greatest
Of funeral fires; smoke rose
3145 Above the flames, black and thick,
And while the wind blew and the fire
Roared they wept, and Beowulf's body
Crumbled and was gone. The Geats stayed,
Moaning their sorrow, lamenting their lord;
3150 A gnarled old woman, hair wound
Tight and gray on her head, groaned
A song of misery, of infinite sadness
And days of mourning, of fear and sorrow
To come, slaughter and terror and captivity.
3155 And Heaven swallowed the billowing smoke.
    Then the Geats built the tower, as Beowulf
Had asked, strong and tall, so sailors
Could find it from far and wide; working
For ten long days they made his monument,
3160 Sealed his ashes in walls as straight
And high as wise and willing hands
Could raise them. And the riches he and
    Wiglaf
Had won from the dragon, rings, necklaces,
Ancient, hammered armor—all
3165 The treasures they'd taken were left there,
    too,
Silver and jewels buried in the sandy
Ground, back in the earth, again
And forever hidden and useless to men.
And then twelve of the bravest Geats
3170 Rode their horses around the tower,
Telling their sorrow, telling stories
Of their dead king and his greatness, his
    glory,
Praising him for heroic deeds, for a life

As noble as his name. So should all men
3175 Raise up words for their lords, warm
With love, when their shield and protector
        leaves
His body behind, sends his soul
On high. And so Beowulf's followers
Rode, mourning their belovèd leader,
3180 Crying that no better king had ever
Lived, no prince so mild, no man
So open to his people, so deserving of praise.

THE END

Glossary of Names

Persons, peoples, and places, are here alphabetically arranged according to the form used in this translation. For those familiar with the original, the Old English spelling is also given, in parentheses and italics.

Not all the names mentioned by the poet are here listed. For a variety of esthetic considerations this translation contains a few alternative identifications; there are a few deletions; and for the most part Danes are Danes and Swedes are Swedes, though (for esthetic reasons valid in his language) the poet may describe them as Spear-Danes, Ring-Danes, East-Danes, North-Danes, or West-Danes. No major omissions occur, however, even under the considerable pressure exerted by such as *Ongenþeow, Hygelac,* and *Wealhþeow.*

BEO (*Beowulf*): a Danish king, Shild's son, Healfdane's father. According to Klaeber, "this form of the name is an error for *Bēow.*" To minimize confusion, I have quietly corrected the poet.

BEOWULF (*Beowulf, Biowulf*): Possibly mythical son of Edgetho, Higlac's nephew and follower, and later king of the Geats. Following the chronology implicit in the poem, Beowulf was born in A.D. 495, went to Denmark and to Hrothgar's help in 515, accompanied Higlac on his expedition against the Franks and Frisians in 521, became king of the Geats in 533, and died at some indefinite later date. The "fifty years" of his reign are, as Klaeber notes, only "a sort of poetic formula."

BONSTAN (*Beanstan, Banstan, Beahstan*): father of Brecca.

BRECCA (*Breca*): chief of a tribe known as the Brondings; a contemporary and young companion of Beowulf. His father is Bonstan.

BRONDINGS (*Brondingas*): a (Scandinavian?) tribe about whom nothing, including their location, seems to be known.

BROSING (*Brosinga*): possibly a reference to Breisach, on the Rhine near Freiburg; possibly a reference to the Brisings, who made a marvelous necklace for the goddess Freyja (see the Norse Elder Edda).

DAGREF (*Dæghrefn*): a Frank warrior, Higlac's killer, who is killed by Beowulf.

ECGLAF (*Ecglaf*): Unferth's father.

EDGETHO (*Ecgþeow*): Beowulf's father, a notable warrior married to Hrethel's one daughter (Beowulf's mother is never named).

EFOR (*Eofor*): a Geat warrior, who kills Ongentho, the Swedish king, and is given Higlac's daughter as a reward.

EMER (*Eomer*): son of Offa.

ERMLAF (*Yrmenlaf*): a Danish nobleman, younger brother of Esher.

ERMRIC (*Eormenric*): a king of the East Goths, historical but converted into the very model of a medieval tyrant; he is so portrayed in the Old English poems "Deor" and "Widsith."

ESHER (*Æschere*): a Danish nobleman, high in the councils of King Hrothgar, and long his close and trusted friend. Esher is killed by Grendel's mother.

FINN (*Finn*): a Frisian king, married to Hnaf's sister.

FITLA (*Fitela*): son (and nephew) of Siegmund. His role, in this and other similar stories, is quite dissimilar to that of Siegfried, who is Siegmund's son (and nephew) in the *Nibelungenlied* and in the Wagner operas.

FRANKS (*Francan*): a West German people, resident near the Rhine and the Meuse rivers. A Frankish tribe conquered Gaul, about A.D. 500, and gave its name to modern France.

FREAW (*Freawaru*): a Danish princess, Hrothgar's daughter. She is given in marriage to Ingeld, a Hathobard prince, in the vain hope of settling the feud between the two peoples.

FRISIANS (*Fresan, Frysan*): a West German people, resident in what is now northwestern Holland.

FRODA (*Froda*): chief of the Hathobards, Ingeld's father.

GARMUND (*Garmund*): Offa's father.

GEATS (*Geatas, Geotena*): a people of southern Sweden, the Gōtar, conquered by the Swedish kingdom in about the sixth century A.D. Infinite ink has been spilled about the precise identification of this people, and their homeland; any and all Old English editions of *Beowulf* (or a fine compendium like R. W. Chambers' *Beowulf*) can lead the interested reader as far as—and probably further than—he cares to go.

GOTHS (*Gifðas*): I have here substituted the well-known Goths for their virtually unknown cousins, the *Gifðas*. The latter tribe emigrated from lands near the mouth of the Vistula (a river in Poland) about the third century A.D., settled near the lower Danube, and were wiped out as an independent political entity by the Lombards, toward the end of the sixth century A.D.

GRENDEL (*Grendel*): a man-eating monster who terrorizes the Danes until killed by Beowulf. Grendel lives, with his equally monstrous mother, at the bottom of a foul lake inhabited by assorted other monsters; he is descended from Cain (the progenitor of all evil spirits), though his precise genealogy is not given. The etymology of his name is conjectural: it is perhaps related to Old Norse *grindill*, "storm," and *grenja*, "to bellow," and to other words meaning "sand," "ground (bottom) of a body of water," and "grinder (destroyer)."

HALGA (*Halga*): a Danish prince, third son of Healfdane, younger brother of King Hrothgar, and father of Hrothulf. Halga predeceased king Hrothgar by some twenty years. The epithet "good" may have been given him for strictly metrical reasons; nothing in the poem explains it.

HAMA (*Hama*): a character in the cycle of stories about Ermric (and Theodoric, not mentioned in *Beowulf*). Precisely what role Hama is supposed to have played, in the poem's oblique reference to him, is not understood.

HARETH (*Hæreð*): Higd's father, apparently a prosperous man of standing.

HATHCYN (*Hæðcyn*): a king of the Geats, Hrethel's second son, who ascends the throne after he accidentally kills his older brother, Herbald, and their father has died of grief. Hathcyn is killed by Ongentho, king of the Swedes, in a war which then sees Ongentho killed by a second band of Geats, led by Higlac.

HATHLAF (*Heaþolaf*): a Wulfing warrior, slain by Edgetho; his death causes a feud which is settled, after Edgetho has been exiled, by the intercession (and gold) of Hrothgar.

HATHOBARDS (*Heaðobeardan*): a seafaring German tribe, sometimes identified with the Lombards (who had not yet migrated down toward Italy), sometimes with the Erulians, but not definitely placed either historically or geographically. They may have lived, at least for a time, on the south Baltic coast.

HEALFDANE (*Healfdene*): a Danish king, Beo's son, and father of Hergar, Hrothgar, Halga, and Urs. Whether or not the name means Half-Dane is uncertain.

HEMMING (*Hemming*): a kinsman of Offa, though in what precise relationship is not known.

HENGEST (*Hengest*): a Danish warrior, Hnaf's chief lieutenant and, de facto, his successor.

HERBALD (*Herebeald*): a prince of the Geats, Hrethel's oldest son. He is killed, in a hunting accident, by his brother, Hathcyn, and his necessarily unavenged death causes his father to die of grief. The parallel with the Balder (Baldr) myth has often been noted.

HERDRED (*Heardred*): a king of the Geats, Higlac's son, killed by the powerful Swedish king, Onela.

HERGAR (*Heorogar*): a Danish king, oldest son of Healfdane, older brother and predecessor of Hrothgar, and father of Herward. His reign was apparently a brief one.

HERMOD (*Heremod*): an archetypal but partly historical Danish king, of great military prowess combined with the lowest possible character. Like Wayland, the famous smith, Hermod is mentioned frequently in the poetry of other Germanic languages.

HEROT (*Heorot*): the lofty battle hall built by King Hrothgar, to celebrate his victories, house his growing band of followers, and perhaps to perpetuate his fame. As the poet hints, in lines 84–85, a coming war will result in the burning down of Herot.

HERWARD (*Heoroweard*): Hergar's son. He seems to have been by-passed, at his father's death (his uncle Hrothgar taking the throne), either because he was thought too young to rule or because he had been out of favor with his father. See lines 2160–2162, and see under Hrothulf, below.

HIGD (*Hygd*): Higlac's wife, Hareth's daughter. Her name means "thoughtful," or "prudent."

HIGLAC (*Hygelac, Higelac*): a king of the Geats, Hrethel's son, younger brother of Herbald and Hathcyn. Higlac is both Beowulf's feudal lord and his uncle.

HNAF (*Hnæf*): a Danish king, killed by Finn; his sister was Finn's wife.

HONDSHEW (*Hondscioh*): a Geat warrior, one of Beowulf's companions on the journey to King Hrothgar's court. Hondshew is the man killed and eaten by Grendel, on the evening when the Geats instead of the Danes lay sleeping in Herot, Hrothgar's hall—the evening when Beowulf, instead of becoming the monster's second victim, gave Grendel his mortal wound.

HRETHEL (*Hreðel*): a king of the Geats, Higlac's father, Beowulf's grandfather.

HRETHRIC (*Hreðric*): the older of Hrothgar's two young sons.

HROTHGAR (*Hroðgar*): a Danish king, second son of Healfdane, builder of Herot, and beneficiary of Beowulf's courage. One of the principal characters of the poem, he is depicted as near the end of his life, wise, brave, but troubled, remembering his glorious past, afflicted with first Grendel and then Grendel's monstrous mother, and worried about the fate of his sons, at his nephew Hrothulf's hands, after his imminent death. Hrothgar has befriended Beowulf's father, which more than satisfactorily accounts for the help Beowulf gives him.

HROTHMUND (*Hroðmund*): the younger of Hrothgar's two young sons.

HROTHULF (*Hroðulf*): Halga's son, Hrothgar's nephew. Although Welthow, Hrothgar's queen, invokes the spirit of good will prevailing at the Danish court, and predicts that Hrothulf will guard her two young sons, the Anglo-Saxon listener knew that Hrothulf was later to seize the throne, after Hrothgar's death, and also was to murder Hrethric, Hrothgar's legal heir. Hrothulf, the Anglo-Saxon listener knew further, was subsequently to be killed by Hergar's son, Herward—but none of this is stated in the poem.

HRUNTING (*Hrunting*): Unferth's ancient sword. Few things show more clearly the importance of weapons (and armor), in Anglo-Saxon culture, than their being assigned names—and, on occasion, other personalized characteristics.

INGELD (*Ingeld*): a prince of the Hathobards, Froda's son, married to Freaw, the Danish princess.

JUTES (*Eotan*): a Frisian people, or a people allied with (and possibly subordinate to?) the Frisians.

NAGLING (*Nægling*): the name of Beowulf's sword. See under Hrunting, above.

OFFA (*Offa*): a king of the Angles—those of them who did not migrate to Angle-land (England) but remained on the European continent. Offa is the husband and tamer of Thrith. Various historical and mythological narratives are fused in this briefly told tale (see also the Old English poem "Widsith").

ONELA (*Onela*): a Swedish king, younger son of Ongentho, and husband of the Danish king Healfdane's daughter. Onela seized the Swedish throne, after his older brother's death; his brother's sons fled to Herdred, king of the Geats. The Swedish king thereupon invaded Geatland, killed Herdred and the older of his two nephews (the legal heir to the Swedish throne), but then returned home and permitted Beowulf to rule Geatland. However, Beowulf soon supported an invasion of Sweden by the surviving nephew, and the latter took both Onela's life and his throne. The poet regards Onela as something of a model king.

ONGENTHO (*Ongenþeow*): a Swedish king, mighty in battle, and obviously respected by the poet. In the fighting which followed Hrethel's death, Ongentho first killed Hathcyn, the Geats' king, and was then himself killed by another group of Geats, led by Higlac. Ongentho is Onela's father.

RENNSBURG (*Hreosnabeorh*): the location of the battle between Swedes and Geats, in which first Hathcyn and then Ongentho are killed.

SHILD (*Scyld*): a Danish king, Beo's father, Healfdane's grandfather, and Hrothgar's great-grandfather. Shild is mythological; he has Scandinavian analogues, as Skjǫldr, and scholars have elaborated a variety of possible religious/agricultural meanings for his story.

SIEGMUND (*Sigemund*): son of Vels, father (and uncle) of Fitla. This is the *Nibelungenlied* (and Wagner's) Siegmund in one of his assorted other incarnations.

SWERTING (*Swerting*): Higlac's grandfather.

THRITH (*Þryð, Modþryðo*): Offa's wife, and a type of haughty, violent young woman very like Katharina, in Shakespeare's *The Taming of the Shrew*. Like Katharina, Thrith is tamed and gentled by a husband stronger even than she; unlike *The Taming of the Shrew*, the poem does not tell us precisely how the miracle was accomplished.

UNFERTH (*Unferð*): one of Hrothgar's courtiers, skillful with words, and also a man of considerable reputation as a warrior; his father is Ecglaf. Unferth's sword, lent to Beowulf for the fight with Grendel's mother, is called Hrunting.

VELS (*Wæls*): Siegmund's father. The familial name is, in this version of the story, derived from Vǫlsung, in the Norse saga.

WAYLAND (*Weland*): a smith celebrated in many surviving Germanic poems; to ascribe a sword or a mail shirt to his gifted hammer was to evoke an automatic association of wonderful workmanship and, in most cases, also of wonderful men and deeds. Wayland is mentioned at some length in "Deor," perhaps the oldest surviving Old English poem (see Raffel, *Poems from the Old English* [1960], pp. 39–40).

WELTHOW (*Wealhþeow*): Hrothgar's queen, and the mother of his young sons, Hrethric and Hrothmund. Most of her speeches are full of tragic implications, well-known to the Anglo-Saxon audience. See under Hrothulf, above.

WEXSTAN (*Wihstan, Weohstan*): Wiglaf's father, and more or less vaguely related to Beowulf. Wexstan killed the older of Onela's nephews, when that Swedish king invaded Geatland, but whether he was himself a Swede, or a Geat serving the Swedes, is not known. In any case, after the survivor of Onela's two nephews returned to Sweden, killed Onela, and became king, Wexstan could not (and did not) remain in Sweden.

WIGLAF (*Wiglaf*): a Geat warrior, more or less vaguely related to Beowulf, possibly having some Swedish blood; his father is Wexstan. Chosen to accompany Beowulf to the aged hero's fight with the dragon, Wiglaf is the only member of a presumably select band who goes to Beowulf's help. He seems to have become king, after Beowulf's death.

WULF (*Wulf*): a Geat warrior, Efor's brother.

WULFGAR (*Wulfgar*): Hrothgar's herald. The precise familial link which leads the poet to call him "a prince born to the Swedes" (*þæt wæs Wendla leod*) is missing.

WULFINGS (*Wylfingas*): a Germanic tribe, probably resident south of the Baltic Sea. Welthow, Hrothgar's queen, may have been a Wulfing.

YRS (*Yrse*): daughter of Healfdane. Her name is not actually given in the manuscript; despite the high degree of probability, editors have hesitated to fill the gap with anything more than [ ] and a footnote. A translator must either gamble or evade.

Related Readings

CONTENTS

The Wanderer

Translated by Burton Raffel

For warriors like Beowulf, life centered around a lord, or king. To be cut off from one's lord was to lose identity, comradeship, protection, and a home. In this poem, dating from the eighth century, the speaker is a warrior whose lord and comrades have been killed and who is forced to flee into lonely exile. What do the memories and yearnings of this wanderer reveal about the experiences of Anglo-Saxon warriors?

This lonely traveller longs for grace,
For the mercy of God; grief hangs on
His heart and follows the frost-cold foam
He cuts in the sea, sailing endlessly,
5 Aimlessly, in exile. Fate has opened
A single port: memory. He sees
His kinsmen slaughtered again, and cries:
       "I've drunk too many lonely dawns,
Grey with mourning. Once there were men
10 To whom my heart could hurry, hot
With open longing. They're long since dead.
My heart has closed on itself, quietly
Learning that silence is noble and sorrow
Nothing that speech can cure. Sadness
15 Has never driven sadness off;
Fate blows hardest on a bleeding heart.
So those who thirst for glory smother
Secret weakness and longing, neither
Weep nor sigh nor listen to the sickness
20 In their souls. So I, lost and homeless,

Forced to flee the darkness that fell
On the earth and my lord.

                                    Leaving everything.
Weary with winter I wandered out
25 On the frozen waves, hoping to find
A place, a people, a lord to replace
My lost ones. No one knew me, now,
No one offered comfort, allowed
Me feasting or joy. How cruel a journey
30 I've travelled, sharing my bread with sorrow
Alone, an exile in every land,
Could only be told by telling my footsteps.
For who can hear: "friendless and poor,"
And know what I've known since the long
    cheerful nights
35 When, young and yearning, with my lord I yet
    feasted
Most welcome of all. That warmth is dead.
He only knows who needs his lord
As I do, eager for long-missing aid;
He only knows who never sleeps
40 Without the deepest dreams of longing.
Sometimes it seems I see my lord,
Kiss and embrace him, bend my hands
And head to his knee, knealing as though
He still sat enthroned, ruling his thanes.
45 And I open my eyes, embracing the air,
And see the brown sea-billows heave,
See the sea-birds bathe, spreading
Their white-feathered wings, watch the frost
And the hail and the snow. And heavy in heart
50 I long for my lord, alone and unloved.
Sometimes it seems I see my kin
And greet them gladly, give them welcome,
The best of friends. They fade away,
Swimming soundlessly out of sight,

55 Leaving nothing.
                              How loathsome become
        The frozen waves to a weary heart.
                    In this brief world I cannot wonder
        That my mind is set on melancholy,
60 Because I never forget the fate
        Of men, robbed of their riches, suddenly
        Looted by death—the doom of earth,
        Sent to us all by every rising
        Sun. Wisdom is slow, and comes
65 But late. He who has it is patient;
        He cannot be hasty to hate or speak,
        He must be bold and yet not blind,
        Nor ever too craven, complacent, or
            covetous,
        Nor ready to gloat before he wins glory.
70 The man's a fool who flings his boasts
        Hotly to the heavens, heeding his spleen
        And not the better boldness of knowledge.
        What knowing man knows not the ghostly,
        Waste-like end of worldly wealth:
75 See, already the wreckage is there,
        The wind-swept walls stand far and wide,
        The storm-beaten blocks besmeared with
            frost,
        The mead-halls crumbled, the monarchs
            thrown down
        And stripped of their pleasures. The proudest
            of warriors
80 Now lie by the wall: some of them war
        Destroyed; some the monstrous sea-bird
        Bore over the ocean; to some the old wolf
        Dealt out death; and for some dejected
        Followers fashioned an earth-cave coffin.
85 Thus the Maker of men lays waste
        This earth, crushing our callow mirth.

And the work of old giants stands withered
and still."

He who these ruins rightly sees,
And deeply considers this dark twisted life,
90   Who sagely remembers the endless slaughters
Of a bloody past, is bound to proclaim:
"Where is the war-steed? Where is the
warrior?
Where is his war-lord?
Where now the feasting-places? Where now
the meadhall pleasures?
Alas, bright cup! Alas, brave knight!
95   Alas, you glorious princes! All gone,
Lost in the night, as you never had lived.
And all that survives you a serpentine wall,
Wondrously high, worked in strange ways.
Mighty spears have slain these men,
100   Greedy weapons have framed their fate.
These rocky slopes are beaten by
storms,
This earth pinned down by driving snow,
By the horror of winter, smothering warmth
In the shadows of night. And the north
angrily
105   Hurls its hailstorms at our helpless heads.
Everything earthly is evilly born,
Firmly clutched by a fickle Fate.
Fortune vanishes, friendship vanishes,
Man is fleeting, woman is fleeting,
110   And all this earth rolls into emptiness."

So says the sage in his heart, sitting
alone with
His thought.

It's good to guard your faith, nor let your
    grief come forth
Until it cannot call for help, nor help but
    heed
The path you've placed before it. It's good to
    find your grace
115 In God, the heavenly rock where rests our
    every hope.

Beowulf

by Richard Wilbur

*Beowulf's feats of extraordinary courage,
strength, and prowess mark him as a hero
for both the Danes and the Geats. The
relationship between a great hero and the
people who revere him may not be simple
or easily understood, however. As you
read this poem by a contemporary
American author, decide whether you
agree with his interpretation of Beowulf's
life and the people he championed.*

The land was overmuch like scenery,
The flowers attentive, the grass too garrulous
    green;
In the lake like a dropped kerchief could be
    seen
The lark's reflection after the lark was gone;
5 The Roman road lay paved too shiningly
For a road so many men had traveled on.

Also the people were strange, were strangely
    warm.
The king recalled the father of his guest,
The queen brought mead in a studded cup,
    the rest
10 Were kind, but in all was a vagueness and a
    strain,
Because they lived in a land of daily harm.
And they said the same things again and
    again.

It was a childish country; and a child,
Grown monstrous, so besieged them in the
    night
15 That all their daytimes were a dream of
    fright
That it would come and own them to the
    bone.
The hero, to his battle reconciled,
Promised to meet that monster all alone.

So then the people wandered to their sleep
20 And left him standing in the echoed hall.
They heard the rafters rattle fit to fall,
The child departing with a broken groan,
And found their champion in a rest so deep
His head lay harder sealed than any stone.

25 The land was overmuch like scenery,
The lake gave up the lark, but now its song
Fell to no ear, the flowers too were wrong,
The day was fresh and pale and swiftly old,
The night put out no smiles upon the sea;
30 And the people were strange, the people
    strangely cold.

They gave him horse and harness, helmet and
    mail,
A jeweled shield, an ancient battle-sword,
Such gifts as are the hero's hard reward
And bid him do again what he has done.
35 These things he stowed beneath his parting
    sail,
And wept that he could share them with no
    son.

He died in his own country a kinless king,
A name heavy with deeds, and mourned as
    one
Will mourn for the frozen year when it is
    done.
40   They buried him next the sea on a thrust of
    land:
Twelve men rode round his barrow all in a
    ring,
Singing of him what they could understand.

from **Grendel**

by John Gardner

Although an ancient work of literature,
Beowulf *still fascinates readers today.*
Modern scholar and writer John Gardner,
steeped in knowledge of early English
poetry, wrote an entire novel based on the
epic—but with a twist: the narrator is
Grendel. This chapter from the novel
begins as Grendel enters the mead hall,
where he will have his fatal encounter
with the Germanic hero.

I touch the door with my fingertips and it bursts, for all its fire-forged bands—it jumps away like a terrified deer—and I plunge into the silent, hearthlit hall with a laugh that I wouldn't much care to wake up to myself. I trample the planks that a moment before protected the hall like a hand raised in horror to a terrified mouth (sheer poetry, ah!) and the broken hinges rattle like swords down the timbered walls. The Geats are stones, and whether it's because they're numb with terror or stiff from too much mead, I cannot tell. I am swollen with excitement, bloodlust and joy and a strange fear that mingle in my chest like the twisting rage of a bone-fire. I step onto the brightly shining floor and angrily advance on them. They're all asleep, the whole company! I can hardly believe my luck and my wild heart laughs, but I let out no sound. Swiftly, softly, I will move from bed to bed and destroy them all, swallow every last man. I am blazing, half-crazy with joy. For pure, mad prank, I snatch a cloth from the nearest table and tie it around my neck to make a napkin. I delay no longer. I seize up a sleeping man, tear at him hungrily, bite through his bone-locks and suck hot, slippery blood. He goes down in huge morsels, head, chest, hips, legs, even the hands and feet. My face and arms are wet, matted. The napkin is sopping. The dark floor steams. I move on at once and I reach for another one (whispering, whispering, chewing the universe down to words), and I seize a wrist. A shock goes through me. Mistake!

It's a trick! His eyes are open, were open all the time, cold-bloodedly watching to see how I work. The eyes nail me now as his hand nails down my arm. I jump back without thinking (whispering wildly: *jump back without thinking*). Now he's out of his bed, his hand still closed like a dragon's jaws on mine. Nowhere on middle-earth, I realize, have I encountered a grip like his. My whole arm's on fire, incredible, searing pain—it's as if his crushing fingers are charged like fangs with poison. I scream, facing him, grotesquely shaking hands—dear long-lost brother, kinsman-thane—and the timbered hall screams back at me. I feel the bones go, ground from their sockets, and I scream again. I am suddenly awake. The long pale dream, my history, falls away. The meadhall is alive, great cavernous belly, gold-adorned, bloodstained, howling back at me, lit by the flickering fire in the stranger's eyes. He has wings. Is it possible? And yet it's true: out of his shoulders come terrible fiery wings. I jerk my head, trying to drive out illusion. The world is what it is and always was. That's our hope, our chance. Yet even in times of catastrophe we people it with tricks. Grendel, Grendel, hold fast to what is true!

Suddenly, darkness. My sanity has won. He's only a man; I can escape him. I plan. I feel the plan moving inside me like thaw-time waters rising between cliffs. When I'm ready, I give a ferocious kick—but something's wrong: I am spinning—Wa!—falling through bottomless space—Wa!—snatching at the huge twisted roots of an oak . . . a blinding flash of fire . . . no, darkness. I concentrate. I have fallen! Slipped on blood. He viciously twists my arm behind my back. By accident, it comes to me, I have given him a greater advantage. I could laugh. *Woe, woe!*

And now something worse. He's whispering— spilling words like showers of sleet, his mouth three inches from my ear. I will not listen. I continue whispering. As long as I whisper myself I need not hear. His syllables lick at me, chilly fire. His syllables lick at me, chilly fire. His syllables lick at me, chilly fire. His syllables lick . . .

A meaningless swirl in the stream of time, a temporary gathering of bits, a few random specks, a cloud . . . Complexities: green dust, purple dust, gold. Additional refinements: sensitive dust, copulating dust . . .

The world is my bone-cave, I shall not want . . . (He laughs as he whispers. I roll my eyes back. Flames slip out at the corners of his mouth.) *As you see it is, while the seeing lasts, dark nightmare-history, time-as-coffin; but where the water was rigid there will be fish, and men will survive on their flesh till spring. It's coming, my brother. Believe it or not. Though you murder the world, turn plains to stone, transmogrify life into I and it, strong searching roots will crack your cave and rain will cleanse it: The world will burn green, sperm build again. My promise. Time is the mind, the hand that makes (fingers on harpstrings, hero-swords, the acts, the eyes of queens). By that I kill you.*

I do not listen. I am sick at heart. I have been

betrayed before by talk like that. "Mama!" I bawl. Shapes vague as lurking seaweed surround us. My vision clears. The stranger's companions encircle us, useless swords. I could laugh if it weren't for the pain that makes me howl. And yet I address him, whispering, whimpering, whining.

"If you win, it's by mindless chance. Make no mistake. First you tricked me, and then I slipped. Accident."

He answers with a twist that hurls me forward screaming. The thanes make way. I fall against a table and smash it, and wall timbers crack. And still he whispers.

Grendel, Grendel! You make the world by whispers, second by second. Are you blind to that? Whether you make it a grave or a garden of roses is not the point. Feel the wall: is it not hard? He smashes me against it, breaks open my forehead. *Hard, yes! Observe the hardness, write it down in careful runes. Now sing of walls! Sing!*

I howl.

Sing!

"I'm singing!"

Sing words! Sing raving hymns!

"You're crazy. Ow!"

Sing!

"I sing of walls," I howl. "Hooray for the hardness of walls!"

Terrible, he whispers. *Terrible.* He laughs and lets out fire.

"You're crazy," I say. "If you think I created that wall that cracked my head, you're a . . . lunatic."

Sing walls, he hisses.

I have no choice.

"The wall will fall to the wind as the windy hill

will fall, and all things thought in former times:
Nothing made remains, nor man remembers.
And these towns shall be called the shining towns!"

Better, he whispers. *That's better.* He laughs again, and the nasty laugh admits I'm slyer than he guessed.

He's crazy. I understand him all right, make no mistake. Understand his lunatic theory of matter and mind, the chilly intellect, the hot imagination, blocks and builder, reality as stress. Nevertheless, it was by accident that he got my arm behind me. He penetrated no mysteries. He was lucky. If I'd known he was awake, if I'd known there was blood on the floor when I gave him that kick . . .

The room goes suddenly white, as if struck by lightning. I stare down, amazed. He has torn off my arm at the shoulder! Blood pours down where the limb was. I cry, I bawl like a baby. He stretches his blinding white wings and breathes out fire. I run for the door and through it. I move like wind. I stumble and fall, get up again. I'll die! I howl. The night is aflame with winged men. *No, no! Think!* I come suddenly awake once more from the nightmare. Darkness. I really will die! Every rock, every tree, every crystal of snow cries out cold-blooded objectness. Cold, sharp outlines, everything around me: distinct, detached as dead men. I understand. "Mama!" I bellow. "Mama, Mama! I'm dying!" But her love is history. His whispering follows me into the woods, though I've outrun him. "It was an accident," I bellow back. I will cling to what is true. "Blind, mindless, mechanical. Mere logic of chance." I am weak from loss of blood. No one follows me now. I stumble again and with my one weak arm I cling to the huge twisted roots of an oak. I look down past stars to a terrifying darkness. I seem to recognize the place, but it's impossible. "Accident," I whisper. I will fall. I seem to desire the fall, and though I fight it with all my will I know in advance that I can't win. Standing baffled, quaking with fear, three feet from the edge of a nightmare cliff, I find myself, incredibly, moving toward it. I look down, down, into bottomless blackness, feeling the dark power moving in me like an ocean current, some monster inside me, deep sea wonder, dread night monarch astir in his cave, moving me slowly to my voluntary tumble into death.

Again sight clears. I am slick with blood. I discover I no longer feel pain. Animals gather around me, enemies of old, to watch me die. I give them what I hope will appear a sheepish smile. My heart booms terror. Will the last of my life slide out if I let out breath? They watch with mindless, indifferent eyes, as calm and midnight black as the chasm below me.

Is it joy I feel?

They watch on, evil, incredibly stupid, enjoying my destruction.

"Poor Grendel's had an accident," I whisper. *"So may you all."*

Beowulf

by Maurice Sagoff

When a piece of literature becomes a cultural monument, it's tempting to have a bit of fun with it. This little parody is from a book called ShrinkLits: Seventy of the World's Towering Classics Cut Down to Size. *Notice how it somehow manages to get everything in.*

Monster Grendel's tastes are plainish.
Breakfast? Just a couple Danish.

King of Danes is frantic, very.
Wait! Here comes the Malmö ferry

5   Bringing Beowulf, his neighbor,
Mighty swinger with a saber!

Hrothgar's warriors hail the Swede,
Knocking back a lot of mead;

Then, when night engulfs the Hall
10 And the Monster makes his call,

Beowulf, with body-slam
Wrenches off his arm, Shazam!

Monster's mother finds him slain,
Grabs and eats another Dane!

15 Down her lair our hero jumps,
Gives old Grendel's dam her lumps.

Later on, as king of Geats
He performed prodigious feats

Till he met a foe too tough
20   (Non-Beodegradable stuff)

And that scaly-armored dragon
Scooped him up and fixed his wagon.

Sorrow-stricken, half the nation
Flocked to Beowulf's cremation;
25   Round his pyre, with drums a-muffle
Did a Nordic soft-shoe shuffle.

from **Gilgamesh**

Translated by Herbert Mason

*The Gilgamesh epic, parts of which date
back 3,000 years, tells the struggles and
triumphs of the hero Gilgamesh, a king of
ancient Sumeria (now modern Iraq). In
this excerpt, Gilgamesh takes on a
legendary monster in battle. Unlike
Beowulf, who fights Grendel alone,
Gilgamesh takes his best friend, Enkidu,
with him on his adventure. As the excerpt
begins, Gilgamesh is announcing to
Enkidu his intention to kill the monster of
the forest, Humbaba.*

Gilgamesh spoke then:
We go to kill the Evil One,
Humbaba. We must prove
Ourselves more powerful than he.

5   Enkidu was afraid of the forest of Humbaba
And urged him not to go, but he
Was not as strong as Gilgamesh in argument,
And they were friends:
They had embraced and made their vow
10   To stay together always,
No matter what the obstacle.
Enkidu tried to hold his fear
But he was sick at heart:
I feel the weakness that I felt before
15   Come over my body, as if I tried to lift
My arms and found that they were hollow.

It is Humbaba who has taken your strength,
Gilgamesh spoke out, anxious
For the journey. We must kill him
20 And end his evil power over us.

No, Enkidu cried; it is the journey
That will take away our life.

Don't be afraid, said Gilgamesh.
We are together. There is nothing
25 We should fear.

I learned, Enkidu said, when I lived
With the animals never to go down
Into *that* forest. I learned that there is death
In Humbaba. Why do you want
30 To raise his anger?

Only half listening Gilgamesh thought
Aloud about the cedars he would climb.

How can we climb those cedars?
Enkidu tried to sway his thoughts:
35 Humbaba never sleeps. He is the guardian
Whom Enlil has commanded to protect
The sacred trees by terror. I have learned
His sound is like a flood's sound
Slowly forming in the distance,
40 Then enveloping all other sounds.
Even the cries of animals cannot be heard.
Trees are hushed, the wind
Still moves them back and forth
But noiselessly. As when one senses
45 Violence gathering its force,
Soon there is no sound apart from it,

Not even one's own thoughts in terror.
I have learned that from his mouth springs
    fire
That scorches the earth and in a moment
50   There is nothing left alive,
No tree, no insect, as in a dream
That makes one wake and cry
Out of the pain one cannot find
The source of, out of nothing;
55   One wakes and everything has vanished.
I have learned Humbaba is the face of death.
He hears each insect crawling toward the
    edge
Of the forest; he twitches and it dies.
Do you think he could not hear two men?

60   Why are you worried about death?
Only the gods are immortal anyway,
Sighed Gilgamesh.
What men do is nothing, so fear is never
Justified. What happened to your power
65   That once could challenge and equal mine?
I will go ahead of you, and if I die
I will at least have the reward
Of having people say: He died in war
Against Humbaba. You cannot discourage
    me
70   With fears and hesitations.
I will fight Humbaba,
I will cut down his cedars.
Tell the armorers to build us two-edged
    swords
And double shields and tell them
75   I am impatient and cannot wait long.

Thus Gilgamesh and Enkidu went
Together to the marketplace
To notify the Elders of Uruk
Who were meeting in their senate.
80 They too were talking of Humbaba,
As they often did,
Edging always in their thoughts
Toward the forbidden.

The one you speak of, Gilgamesh addressed
them,
85 I now must meet. I want to prove
Him not the awesome thing we think he is
And that the boundaries set up by gods
Are not unbreakable. I will defeat him
In his cedar forest. The youth of Uruk
90 Need this fight. They have grown soft
And restless.

The old men leaned a little
forward
Remembering old wars. A flush burned on
Their cheeks. It seemed a little dangerous
And yet they saw their king
95 Was seized with passion for this fight.
Their voices gave the confidence his friend
Had failed to give; some even said
Enkidu's wisdom was a sign of cowardice.
You see, my friend, laughed Gilgamesh,
100 The wise of Uruk have outnumbered you.

Amidst the speeches in the hall
That called upon the gods for their
protection,
Gilgamesh saw in his friend that pain

He had seen before and asked him what it
    was
105 That troubled him.

Enkidu could not speak. He held his tears
Back. Barely audibly he said:
It is a road which you have never traveled.

The armorers brought to Gilgamesh his
    weapons
110 And put them in his hand. He took his
    quiver,
Bow and ax, and two-edged sword,
And they began to march.

The Elders gave their austere blessing
And the people shouted: Let Enkidu lead,
115 Don't trust your strength, he knows the
    forests,
The one who goes ahead will save his friend.
May Shamash bring you victory.

Enkidu was resolved to lead his friend
Who was determined but did not know the
    way.
120 Now Gilgamesh was certain with his friend
Beside him. They went to Ninsun, his mother,
Who would advise them how to guard their
    steps.
Her words still filled his mind
As they started their journey,
125 Just as a mother's voice is heard
Sometimes in a man's mind
Long past childhood
Calling his name, calling him from sleep

Or from some pleasureful moment
130   On a foreign street
When every trace of origin seems left
And one has almost passed into a land
That promises a vision or the secret
Of one's life, when one feels almost god
    enough
135   To be free of voices, her voice
Calls out like a voice from childhood,
Reminding him he once tossed in dreams.
He still could smell the incense she had
    burned
To Shamash, saying: Why did you give my
    son
140   A restless heart, and now you touch him
With this passion to destroy Humbaba,
And you send him on a journey to a battle
He may never understand, to a door
He cannot open. You inspire him to end
145   The evil of the world which you abhor
And yet he is a man for all his power
And cannot do your work. You must protect
My son from danger.

                     She had put out the
    incense
And called Enkidu to her side, and said:
150   You are not my son but I adopt you
And call upon the same protection now
For you I called upon for Gilgamesh.
She placed a charm around his neck, and
    said:
O let Enkidu now protect his friend.

155   These words still filled their minds
As the two friends continued on their way.
After three days they reached the edge
Of the forest where Humbaba's watchman
    stood.
Suddenly it was Gilgamesh who was afraid,
160   Enkidu who reminded him to be fearless.
The watchman sounded his warning to
    Humbaba.
The two friends moved slowly toward the
    forest gate.

When Enkidu touched the gate his hand felt
    numb,
He could not move his fingers or his wrist,
165   His face turned pale like someone's witness-
    ing a death,
He tried to ask his friend for help
Whom he had just encouraged to move on,
But he could only stutter and hold out
His paralyzed hand.
170   It will pass, said Gilgamesh.
Would you want to stay behind because of
    that?
We must go down into the forest together.
Forget your fear of death. I will go before
    you
And protect you. Enkidu followed close
    behind
175   So filled with fear he could not think or
    speak.
Soon they reached the high cedars.

They stood in awe at the foot
Of the green mountain. Pleasure
Seemed to grow from fear for Gilgamesh.
180 As when one comes upon a path in woods
Unvisited by men, one is drawn near
The lost and undiscovered in himself;
He was revitalized by danger.
They knew it was the path Humbaba made.
185 Some called the forest "Hell," and others
        "Paradise";
What difference does it make? said
        Gilgamesh.
But night was falling quickly
And they had no time to call it names,
Except perhaps "The Dark,"
190 Before they found a place at the edge of the
        forest
To serve as shelter for their sleep.

It was a restless night for both. One snatched
At sleep and sprang awake from dreams. The
        other
Could not rest because of pain that spread
195 Throughout his side. Enkidu was alone
With sights he saw brought on by pain
And fear, as one in deep despair
May lie beside his love who sleeps
And seems so unafraid, absorbing in himself
        the phantoms
200 That she cannot see—phantoms diminished
        for one
When two can see and stay awake to talk of
        them
And search out a solution to despair,
Or lie together in each other's arms,

Or weep and in exhaustion from their tears
205 Perhaps find laughter for their fears.
But alone and awake the size and nature
Of the creatures in his mind grow
        monstrous, . . .
He cried aloud for them to stop appearing
        over him
Emerging from behind the trees with
        phosphorescent eyes
210 Brought on by rain. He could not hear his
        voice
But knew he screamed and could not move
        his arms
But thought they tried to move
As if a heavy weight he could not raise
Or wriggle out from underneath
215 Had settled on his chest,
Like a turtle trapped beneath a fallen branch,
Each effort only added to paralysis.
He could not make his friend, his one
        companion, hear.

Gilgamesh awoke but could not hear
220 His friend in agony, he still was captive to his
        dreams
Which he would tell aloud to exorcise:
I saw us standing in a mountain gorge,
A rockslide fell on us, we seemed no more
Than insects under it. And then
225 A solitary graceful man appeared
And pulled me out from under the mountain.
He gave me water and I felt released.

Tomorrow you will be victorious,
Enkidu said, to whom the dream brought
    chills

230 (For only one of them, he knew, would be
        released)
Which Gilgamesh could not perceive in the
    darkness
For he went back to sleep without responding
To his friend's interpretation of his dream.
Did you call me? Gilgamesh sat up again.

235 Why did I wake again? I thought you touched
    me.
Why am I afraid? I felt my limbs grow numb
As if some god passed over us drawing out
    our life.
I had another dream:
This time the heavens were alive with fire, but
    soon

240 The clouds began to thicken, death rained
        down on us,
The lightning flashes stopped, and everything
Which rained down turned to ashes.
What does this mean, Enkidu?

That you will be victorious against Humbaba,

245 Enkidu said, or someone said through him
Because he could not hear his voice
Or move his limbs although he thought he
    spoke,
And soon he saw his friend asleep beside him.

At dawn Gilgamesh raised his ax

250 And struck at the great cedar.
When Humbaba heard the sound of falling
    trees,

He hurried down the path that they had seen
But only he had traveled. Gilgamesh felt
   weak
At the sound of Humbaba's footsteps and
   called to Shamash
255 Saying, I have followed you in the way
   decreed;
Why am I abandoned now? Suddenly the
   winds
Sprang up. They saw the great head of
   Humbaba
Like a water buffalo's bellowing down the
   path,
His huge and clumsy legs, his flailing arms
260 Thrashing at phantoms in his precious trees.
His single stroke could cut a cedar down
And leave no mark on him. His shoulders,
Like a porter's under building stones,
Were permanently bent by what he bore;
265 He was the slave who did the work for gods
But whom the gods would never notice.
Monstrous in his contortion, he aroused
The two almost to pity.
But pity was the thing that might have killed.
270 It made them pause just long enough to show
How pitiless he was to them. Gilgamesh in
   horror saw
Him strike the back of Enkidu and beat him
   to the ground
Until he thought his friend was crushed to
   death.
He stood still watching as the monster leaned
   to make
275 His final strike against his friend, unable
To move to help him, and then Enkidu slid

Along the ground like a ram making its final
    lunge
On wounded knees. Humbaba fell and seemed
To crack the ground itself in two, and
    Gilgamesh,
280 As if this fall had snapped him from his daze,
Returned to life
And stood over Humbaba with his ax
Raised high above his head watching the
    monster plead
In strangled sobs and desperate appeals
285 The way the sea contorts under a violent
    squall.
I'll serve you as I served the gods, Humbaba
    said;
I'll build you houses from their sacred trees.

Enkidu feared his friend was weakening
And called out: Gilgamesh! Don't trust him!
290 As if there were some hunger in himself
That Gilgamesh was feeling
That turned him momentarily to yearn
For someone who would serve, he paused;
And then he raised his ax up higher
295 And swung it in a perfect arc
Into Humbaba's neck. He reached out
To touch the wounded shoulder of his friend,

And late that night he reached again
To see if he was yet asleep, but there was only
300 Quiet breathing. The stars against the mid-
    night sky
Were sparkling like mica in a riverbed.
In the slight breeze
The head of Humbaba was swinging from a
    tree.

David and Goliath

from I Samuel, Chapters 16–18
The King James Bible

Beowulf, already a famous hero for his brave deeds, faces unique challenges as he battles Grendel, Grendel's mother, and the dragon. In the ancient story of David and Goliath, the young shepherd David, who has never been in battle, takes on the giant Goliath, a formidable and seasoned warrior. As you read, look for both the parallels between Beowulf and David and the unique challenges each encounters.

Chapter 16

And the Lord said unto Samuel, How long wilt thou mourn for Saul, seeing I have rejected him from reigning over Israel? fill thine horn with oil, and go, I will send thee to Jesse the Bethlehemite: for I have provided me a king among his sons. . . .

10   Again, Jesse made seven of his sons to pass before Samuel. And Samuel said unto Jesse, The Lord hath not chosen these.

11   And Samuel said unto Jesse, Are here all thy children? and he said, There remaineth yet the youngest, and, behold, he keepeth the sheep. And Samuel said unto Jesse, Send and fetch him: for we will not sit down till he come hither.

12   And he sent, and brought him in. Now he was ruddy, and withal of a beautiful countenance, and

goodly to look to. And the Lord said, Arise, anoint him: for this is he.

13 Then Samuel took the horn of oil, and anointed him in the midst of his brethren: and the Spirit of the Lord came upon David from that day forward. So Samuel rose up, and went to Ramah.

14 But the Spirit of the Lord departed from Saul, and an evil spirit from the Lord troubled him.

15 And Saul's servants said unto him, Behold now, an evil spirit from God troubleth thee.

16 Let our lord now command thy servants, which are before thee, to seek out a man, who is a cunning player on an harp: and it shall come to pass, when the evil spirit from God is upon thee, that he shall play with his hand, and thou shalt be well.

17 And Saul said unto his servants, Provide me now a man that can play well, and bring him to me.

18 Then answered one of the servants, and said, Behold, I have seen a son of Jesse the Bethlehemite, that is cunning in playing, and a mighty valiant man, and a man of war, and prudent in matters, and a comely person, and the Lord is with him.

19 Wherefore Saul sent messengers unto Jesse, and said, Send me David thy son, which is with the sheep. . . .

21 And David came to Saul, and stood before him: and he loved him greatly; and he became his armourbearer.

22 And Saul sent to Jesse, saying, Let David, I pray thee, stand before me; for he hath found favour in my sight. . . .

Chapter 17

Now the Philistines gathered together their armies to battle, and were gathered together at Shochoh, which belongeth to Judah, and pitched between Shochoh and Azekah, in Ephesdammim.

2　And Saul and the men of Israel were gathered together, and pitched by the valley of Elah, and set the battle in array against the Philistines.

3　And the Philistines stood on a mountain on the one side, and Israel stood on a mountain on the other side: and there was a valley between them.

4　And there went out a champion out of the camp of the Philistines, named Goliath, of Gath, whose height was six cubits and a span.

5　And he had an helmet of brass upon his head, and he was armed with a coat of mail; and the weight of the coat was five thousand shekels of brass.

6　And he had greaves of brass upon his legs, and a target of brass between his shoulders.

7　And the staff of his spear was like a weaver's beam; and his spear's head weighed six hundred shekels of iron: and one bearing a shield went before him.

8　And he stood and cried unto the armies of Israel, and said unto them, Why are ye come out to set your battle in array? am not I a Philistine, and ye servants to Saul? choose you a man for you, and let him come down to me.

9　If he be able to fight with me, and to kill me, then will we be your servants: but if I prevail against him, and kill him, then shall ye be our servants, and serve us.

10　And the Philistine said, I defy the armies of Israel this day; give me a man, that we may fight together.

11   When Saul and all Israel heard those words of the Philistine, they were dismayed, and greatly afraid.

12   Now David was the son of that Ephrathite of Bethlehemjudah, whose name was Jesse; and he had eight sons: and the man went among men for an old man in the days of Saul.

13   And the three eldest sons of Jesse went and followed Saul to the battle: and the names of his three sons that went to the battle were Eliab the first born, and next unto him Abinadab, and the third Shammah.

14   And David was the youngest: and the three eldest followed Saul.

15   But David went and returned from Saul to feed his father's sheep at Bethlehem.

16   And the Philistine drew near morning and evening, and presented himself forty days.

17   And Jesse said unto David his son, Take now for thy brethren an ephah of this parched corn, and these ten loaves, and run to the camp to thy brethren;

18   And carry these ten cheeses unto the captain of their thousand, and look how thy brethren fare, and take their pledge.

19   Now Saul, and they, and all the men of Israel, were in the valley of Elah, fighting with the Philistines.

20   And David rose up early in the morning, and left the sheep with a keeper, and took, and went, as Jesse had commanded him; and he came to the trench, as the host was going forth to the fight, and shouted for the battle.

21   For Israel and the Philistines had put the battle in array, army against army.

22   And David left his carriage in the hand of the keeper of the carriage, and ran into the army, and came and saluted his brethren.

23   And as he talked with them, behold, there came

up the champion, the Philistine of Gath, Goliath by name, out of the armies of the Philistines, and spake according to the same words: and David heard them.

24 And all the men of Israel, when they saw the man, fled from him, and were sore afraid.

25 And the men of Israel said, Have ye seen this man that is come up? surely to defy Israel is he come up: and it shall be, that the man who killeth him, the king will enrich him with great riches, and will give him his daughter, and make his father's house free in Israel.

26 And David spake to the men that stood by him, saying, What shall be done to the man that killeth this Philistine, and taketh away the reproach from Israel? for who is this uncircumcised Philistine, that he should defy the armies of the living God?

27 And the people answered him after this manner, saying, So shall it be done to the man that killeth him.

28 And Eliab his eldest brother heard when he spake unto the men; and Eliab's anger was kindled against David, and he said, Why camest thou down hither? and with whom hast thou left those few sheep in the wilderness? I know thy pride, and the naughtiness of thine heart; for thou art come down that thou mightest see the battle.

29 And David said, What have I now done? Is there not a cause? . . .

31 And when the words were heard which David spake, they rehearsed them before Saul: and he sent for him.

32 And David said to Saul, Let no man's heart fail because of him; thy servant will go and fight with this Philistine.

33 And Saul said to David, Thou art not able to go against this Philistine to fight with him: for thou art but a youth, and he a man of war from his youth.

34 And David said unto Saul, Thy servant kept his father's sheep, and there came a lion, and a bear, and took a lamb out of the flock:

35 And I went out after him, and smote him, and delivered it out of his mouth: and when he arose against me, I caught him by his beard, and smote him, and slew him.

36 Thy servant slew both the lion and the bear: and this uncircumcised Philistine shall be as one of them, seeing he hath defied the armies of the living God.

37 David said moreover, The Lord that delivered me out of the paw of the lion, and out of the paw of the bear, he will deliver me out of the hand of this Philistine. And Saul said unto David, Go, and the Lord be with thee.

38 And Saul armed David with his armour, and he put an helmet of brass upon his head; also he armed him with a coat of mail.

39 And David girded his sword upon his armour, and he assayed to go; for he had not proved it. And David said unto Saul, I cannot go with these; for I have not proved them. And David put them off him.

40 And he took his staff in his hand, and chose him five smooth stones out of the brook, and put them in a shepherd's bag which he had, even in a scrip; and his sling was in his hand: and he drew near to the Philistine.

41 And the Philistine came on and drew near unto David; and the man that bare the shield went before him.

42 And when the Philistine looked about, and saw David, he disdained him: for he was but a youth, and ruddy, and of a fair countenance.

43 And the Philistine said unto David, Am I a dog, that thou comest to me with staves? And the Philistine cursed David by his gods.

44   And the Philistine said to David, Come to me, and I will give thy flesh unto the fowls of the air, and to the beasts of the field.

45   Then said David to the Philistine, Thou comest to me with a sword, and with a spear, and with a shield: but I come to thee in the name of the Lord of hosts, the God of the armies of Israel, whom thou hast defied.

46   This day will the Lord deliver thee into mine hand; and I will smite thee, and take thine head from thee; and I will give the carcases of the host of the Philistines this day unto the fowls of the air, and to the wild beasts of the earth; that all the earth may know that there is a God in Israel.

47   And all this assembly shall know that the Lord saveth not with sword and spear: for the battle is the Lord's, and he will give you into our hands.

48   And it came to pass, when the Philistine arose, and came and drew nigh to meet David, that David hasted, and ran toward the army to meet the Philistine.

49   And David put his hand in his bag, and took thence a stone, and slang it, and smote the Philistine in his forehead, that the stone sunk into his forehead; and he fell upon his face to the earth.

50   So David prevailed over the Philistine with a sling and with a stone, and smote the Philistine, and slew him; but there was no sword in the hand of David.

51   Therefore David ran, and stood upon the Philistine, and took his sword, and drew it out of the sheath thereof, and slew him, and cut off his head therewith. And when the Philistines saw their champion was dead, they fled.

52   And the men of Israel and of Judah arose, and shouted, and pursued the Philistines, until thou come

to the valley, and to the gates of Ekron. And the wounded of the Philistines fell down by the way to Shaaraim, even unto Gath, and unto Ekron.

53 And the children of Israel returned from chasing after the Philistines, and they spoiled their tents.

54 And David took the head of the Philistine, and brought it to Jerusalem; but he put his armour in his tent.

55 And when Saul saw David go forth against the Philistine, he said unto Abner, the captain of the host, Abner, whose son is this youth? And Abner said, As thy soul liveth, O king, I cannot tell.

56 And the king said, Enquire thou whose son the stripling is.

57 And as David returned from the slaughter of the Philistine, Abner took him, and brought him before Saul with the head of the Philistine in his hand.

58 And Saul said to him, Whose son art thou, thou young man? And David answered, I am the son of thy servant Jesse the Bethlehemite. . . .

Chapter 18

6 And it came to pass as they came, when David was returned from the slaughter of the Philistine, that the women came out of all cities of Israel, singing and dancing, to meet king Saul, with tabrets, with joy, and with instruments of musick.

7 And the women answered one another as they played, and said, Saul hath slain his thousands, and David his ten thousands.

8 And Saul was very wroth, and the saying displeased him; and he said, They have ascribed unto David ten thousands, and to me they have ascribed but thousands: and what can he have more but the kingdom?

Anger

from The Seven Deadly Sins

by Linda Pastan

Crouching in his lair, Grendel knew this emotion well, as did his mother. But anger belongs not only to monsters, as we discover when we look within ourselves. That is what contemporary poet Linda Pastan reveals in this poem.

You tell me
that it's all right
to let it out of its cage,
though it may claw someone,
5   even bite.
You say that letting it out
may tame it somehow.
But loose it may
turn on me, maul
10   my face, draw blood.
Ah, you think you know so much,
you whose anger is a pet dog,
its canines dull with disuse.
But mine is a rabid thing,
15   sharpening its teeth
on my very bones,
and I will never let it go.

from A Gathering of Heroes

by Gregory Alan-Williams

Life in today's world sometimes calls for heroic responses. On April 29, 1992, actor Gregory Alan-Williams was driving down Century Boulevard in South Central Los Angeles, when he heard the news of a jury's acquittal of four white police officers accused of beating a black motorist named Rodney King. Later that day, Alan-Williams heard that there were riots breaking out in his community. He decided to go to the intersection of Florence and Normandie avenues to try to convince people not to harm one another. After parking his car near the intersection and walking to it, he found himself facing a teeming mob, in which people armed with broken bottles, bricks, and rocks were pelting the cars that passed through the intersection. This excerpt is from Alan-Williams's book recounting his experience during the riots. It begins when a brown Ford Bronco, under attack by the mob, stops in the intersection. As you read, compare Alan-Williams's heroism with that of Beowulf.

The windshield on the driver's side of the brown Ford Bronco segued almost invisibly from transparent ocean green to frosty white at the brick's impact. New missiles launched from three of the four street corners were already hurtling toward the two-door four-wheeler as it slammed to a stop. The driver quickly leaned right, locking the passenger door, then slammed home the lock nearest him. For a blink of an eye, it appeared that the truck's other glass barriers would hold, but a beat after the new projectiles ricocheted from them, the brittle panes shattered into a thousand hopeless pieces, and collapsed evenly from the window frame. . . .

A dozen or so people sprinted toward the Bronco sitting motionless in the middle of the intersection, ignoring the debris that flew past their heads toward the now nearly windowless vehicle. . . .

Someone behind me shouted as the first blow stunned the driver in his seat. The bottle came through the driver's side window which had been shattered by a metal-rod-wielding "champion" at point-blank range. Like a starter's pistol, the crack of the glass against the driver's skull launched an onslaught of blows from every direction. Someone crawled through the windowless rear hatch and began beating the driver from behind. A tall slender young man ran from the southwest corner, jumped through the missing passenger window, and commenced a one-handed assault with a glass bottle, his legs dangling outside the cab.

From the first blow, the driver had been unable to protect himself. He was battered about like a sad puppet, his movements subject solely to the direction and momentum of his assailants' rage. Within fifteen or twenty seconds, the man lost consciousness, and slumped forward onto the steering wheel. Immediately, he was driven backward to an upright position by several more blows to the head.

As I watched, this brought home vividly something that had happened to me in junior high school in the spring of 1969. I was in the school auditorium; band practice was almost over, and we were waiting for the sound of the buzzer that would signal our release. I twisted apart my shiny black clarinet, swabbed out the saliva and placed the three sections snugly into the soft burgundy velveteen interior of its case. The buzzer went off. All of us began to move up the aisle of the auditorium toward our lockers to gather up our books and then board the buses for home. I was a few feet from the auditorium doors, engaging in some good-natured banter with another student, when some hard object—like a rock—slammed against my mouth: the flesh burst into bleeding pulp against my teeth. The strength of the blow, combined with the downward incline of the aisle, sent me reeling backward into the students behind me. They parted like the Red Sea. I fell over some seats, righted myself and touched two trembling fingers to the pain in my mouth. I could feel the flesh hanging from where my bottom lip had been.

Dazed and bleeding, I staggered back and forth across the aisle, trying to understand what had happened. I was frightened by the feel of my own blood, wet and sticky on my hands. I caught a blurry glimpse of someone standing laughing in the middle of the aisle. I couldn't make out his face, but he was huge. It turned out later that he was a big eighteen-year-old from a high school several miles away. Some kids were standing at the edges of the aisle, others had gathered up ahead and were watching silently from the double doors of the auditorium. A few joined my assailant in laughter. I careened wildly about the auditorium—a pitiful, helpless, hurt child. I didn't know who my assailant was, or why he had struck me. And I had lost my clarinet. I was hoping desperately that someone in this "enlightened "landscape" would help me. Help me get away from that huge laughing figure, away from my shame and from those who watched me as I staggered about, bloody and afraid. Eventually a teacher came and helped me to the office.

A few days later, as I sat, stitched and swollen, in the vice principal's office, I came to understand what had happened, for the vice principal said that I had come to his school "walking too tall" and holding my head "a little too high" and many of the students resented it. "So," he said to my mother, "of course, what could you expect?"

Only a short time before I had transferred to this school from a predominantly black school in Des Moines, where I had not seemed to fit in: my "ethnicity" had been questioned, so to speak. I wasn't an athlete, I liked to play the piano, and I "talked funny." I thought I would be happier here. Now I was overwhelmed with despair at the discovery that in this Middle-American educational institution—where I was one of two African-American students—I was not respected as a human being. It was not my ethnicity that was questioned, but my humanity. I carried the scar of the incident for twenty-five years—not only physically, but psychologically, because through it I lost a trusted friend. I realized only recently that I haven't played the clarinet since that day in the auditorium.

Now the vivid memory of that beating and abandonment, some twenty-five years ago, propelled me into the intersection. I remembered too well the feelings I had had, the hurtful words and images—I could not accept this attack, the suffering of this human being. It seemed that he and I had become one, that his suffering and mine, present and past, had fused, and with one loud and silent voice now cried for help within this single irretrievable moment.

My conscience heard our cry, and carried me forward to preserve justice for him and to reclaim justice for myself.

I moved neither slowly nor quickly, not in anger but in extreme sorrow. Sorrow for those who were seeing, but who could not see; sorrow for the ones who saw but who had lost the ability to feel; sorrow for the hated and for those who nurtured hate with their silence. Although the man in the intersection was being robbed of his existence, my sorrow was not for death, but for the prevailing misery of life, and grew from a remembrance of the ache that comes with knowing that one has been exiled from the human heart.

"Come on, y'all . . . y'all know this ain't right," I said to several people jockeying for striking positions at the driver's side of the truck. One fellow had his hand on the latch, and was about to open the door. I looked squarely into the eyes of another who had just landed a blow to the driver's face. The bottle he was holding chest high dropped immediately to his side. He took a small step backward, bumping into a short, stout, middle-aged black man, who, with his back and right leg pinned against the vehicle, and his arms outstretched, was trying to hold people back and away from the truck while he pleaded for the driver's life. "Please, please! Don't do this. Please don't hurt him no more!"

The would-be assailant behind me had begun to open the door. With my left hand I gripped the door frame, pushed the door fully open, stepped in between the driver and his attackers, reached inside the cab, and grabbed the unconscious victim under the arms. "Come on man, let's go," I said. I could barely make out, through the blood, that he was of Asian descent.

He was heavy and it took a moment to get a solid grip on him. I pulled hard and held my body against his back in order to ease his drop from the truck cab to the street, my face pressed against his blood-soaked hair. Suddenly the light which was coming through the window frame on the passenger side was blotted out by a large figure leaping head first into the cab. Simultaneously, a glass bottle shattered against the Asian man's face, spraying stinging shards across my left cheek.

For a few brief moments, time seemed to slow down tremendously; I felt as if my body and everything around me was moving at half speed. I had been calm as I walked toward the truck. But now, as I felt the tiny particles of glass clinging to my skin, real time resumed, and adrenaline drove me backward and away from the vehicle with my unconscious and bloody stranger firmly in tow. I was praying that my legs would carry us far enough, fast enough, to escape the next blow.

After seeing the man being so easily jostled around the cab of the truck, I was surprised that his unconscious form was so heavy. Because he was so heavy, we were not moving fast enough to outrun the mob. Six or seven feet from the Bronco, a young man ran toward us, bottle in hand, cocking his arm for a hit. I knew what was coming. With all my strength I tried to turn the driver's limp body away from the direction of the attack. Sadly, I was too slow. The beer bottle disintegrated almost silently against the man's already unrecognizable face.

Anger and revulsion leaped into my throat as I watched his assailant scurry away toward the anonymity of the crowd. I cringed at the youngster's cowardice. . . .

For an instant I wanted to hurt him, as he had hurt

someone else. I wanted to shake him until he woke from the senseless and bitter nightmare that had terrorized his spirit, and so wickedly altered his reality. I wanted to make him understand that he was the seed of a courageous and compassionate people. And, that although his American ancestors were often hard pressed for life's essentials, and sometimes for life itself, he was infinitely poorer than they. Because unlike those before him, he was now a man without honor. I wished that I could force open his eyes, so that he could look clearly at his victim, and see the truth about himself.

My anger subsided, replaced by a sad awareness that the sick and brutal young man might never perceive the spiritual self-destructiveness of his inhumanity. Perhaps in bitter years to come, as he sought to blame others for his discontent, he would somehow come to comprehend that it is most often our own actions which power the wheels of our fate. If he were very lucky, one day he might be shown, as I had been, that the millstone of dishonor often far exceeds the weight of injustice. For dishonor, self-imposed, grates heavily upon the conscience, and crushes the spirit.

I pulled the still-unconscious man to the sidewalk, laid him on the pavement, and held his head in my hands. He appeared to be coming to, so with urgency, I asked, "Can you walk?"

He shook his head. No.

"Well, you gotta walk or you're gonna die," I told him, lifting him back to his feet.

He was more than wobbly, but managed to hold himself up long enough for me to get one arm around his waist, and his right arm over my shoulder. Unable to see for the blood which ran freely into his eyes, semi-conscious and beaten nearly beyond recognition, miraculously he began to put one foot in front of the other as I guided him down the sidewalk. He held on to me the way a drowning man clings to a life preserver. And then he looked at me in a way that seemed so familiar—I had seen it somewhere before, but couldn't place it. The look came from deep within him, a look that said "thanks," and "congratulations," all at once. Suddenly, I experienced a buoyant and peaceful feeling, a mood so confident and gentle that I knew our communion was a celebration of life. And that, if we survived, from this day forward, we would have that life more abundantly.

"What's your name?" I asked him.

I attributed his unintelligible answer to the thickness of a foreign accent and assumed that he was a recent immigrant.

"Welcome to America," I said with a smile. Later I realized that he could not speak because his lips were torn and broken. I also found out later that this American had been born in a government internment camp during the Second World War, and that he had grown up not far from this very street. In response to my mistaken welcome, he raised the one eye which had not swelled shut, and through shattered blood-caked lips, and broken teeth, flashed me a small painful grin.

"Yeah, you Korean . . . got what you deserved, that's for Latasha Harlins!" a teenage girl screamed as she passed to our right on the sidewalk, referring to the Los Angeles teenager who had been killed by a Korean grocer the previous year. The angry girl's companion stood wide-eyed as we approached, then covered her own gaping, speechless mouth with one hand, closed her eyes, and rushed past us, unable to look upon the face of vengeance.

As we moved down the sidewalk, people parted to let us by. Their expressions varied from shock and horror to broad smiles and indifferent stares. Some burst into tears at the sight of the wounded man. Others, calloused by a brutal existence, glanced in our direction, and continued their curbside conversations. . . .

My friend was getting heavier. I needed to find a safe place for a moment's rest. On our right, in the middle of the block, we turned into a driveway that led to a small apartment building which stood in back of the commercial property that fronted the street. To my left, I noticed another building with rear steps which were not visible from Florence. Relieved, I ducked around the corner of the structure and made a move to set my charge down on the concrete stairs. "Hell no!" a voice from behind me hollered. "Get him the hell out of here!" Across the driveway, a small tan-skinned man struck firmly at the air with the back of his hand, gesturing for us to go away. . . .

I figured we had enough trouble, so I didn't argue. I picked my friend up again and headed back out to the street. The man's female companion began to plead with him on our behalf, but he refused to listen. I sensed, however, that her words had affected him, for as we resumed our journey, we passed directly in front of him and even as he continued to order us off his property, he could no longer look at us. He literally turned his back as he drove us away with his fear. . . .

After several minutes, a great shout went up from the corner: a black-and-white police cruiser had passed, headed toward the intersection, and the bystanders were hailing the officers on our behalf. The squad car backed up, turned, and pulled to a stop in front of us. I smiled when I spoke to them, glad that my mission was nearly accomplished. "This guy's hurt bad, he needs help," I said.

The black officer behind the wheel and his white female partner were silent. They stared at us for twenty or thirty seconds; then, without gesture or word, they drove away. Immediately, adrenaline started losing ground to the fear not so deep inside me. I couldn't believe it. I had kept walking in the certainty that eventually, in the midst of this madness, I would run into a cop or a paramedic. And I had been right, but now they were driving away, and I was so stunned I couldn't even cry out after them. I watched as they made a U-turn at the next intersection and headed back toward us. Again they stopped and looked. The black cop was talking on the radio. The female cop, blond with a Gibson Girl hairstyle, looked at us over the ridge of the seat. The male cop was wearing his "street face," but I could tell that the woman officer was concerned. The look on her face said she wanted to help us, but was somehow prevented from doing so. That look stayed on her face, even as her partner pulled off for the second and final time. . . .

With the departure of the officers, it became clear to all that chaos reigned. . . .

In a reality ruled by madmen, mutes, and cowards, I pulled my friend to his feet and contemplated a new journey. Again he began to turn deliriously, this way and that. "Don't move, damn it, just don't move," I demanded. I held him close . . . , locking him in an embrace to keep him motionless. We could not turn back. To go north we would have to cross Florence. Continuing east would take us further from the violence but toward what, I could not be sure. The residential road to the south was empty. As far as I could see there were only locked and quiet homes. No crowds, no traffic, just an occasional weary-looking "revolutionary," sidestepping and glancing over his shoulder as he spirited a case of looted liquor toward some hiding place. So south we went, arm over a shoulder, arm around a waist. We had traveled only a short distance when I noticed the blood flowing dark and steady from my friend's left ear. . . .

I wasn't sure what sort of injury the blood indicated, but at that moment I began to fear that his injuries were threatening his life.

I hoped that the light pole would hide my friend from anyone looking south from Florence long enough for me to figure out what to do. Within seconds a small blue car, full of little brown children, pulled to a stop behind me. A plump brown woman at the wheel leaned past the two children in the front seat and asked, "Do you want me to take him to the hospital?" There was little room left in the car, no way to conceal him except underneath the children. "No, that's okay," I said, "the kids might get hurt."

The woman was still for a moment, then nodded and drove off. As she pulled away, a brown Chevy van rounded the corner from Florence. "Yo man, you want me to take him to the hospital?" asked its lone occupant, a thirtyish black man wearing a black "doo rag" on his head; it hung down to his shoulders.

"Naw . . . that's all right," I said with a frown.

"You sure, partner? He looks like he's hurt pretty bad." The van driver pressed me.

I glanced at the blood still flowing from my semi-conscious friend's ear, then turned back to the driver, "You sure, man? You're gonna take him to the hospital, right?"

The man in the van seemed to appreciate my

uncertainty; he became thoughtful for a moment, then replied, "For real, Black. For real."

I lifted my friend to his feet and carried him to the passenger side of the van. The driver leaned over, opened the door, and together we got him securely into the front seat.

"Thanks," I said to the driver, reaching over to shake his hand.

Acknowledgments

Continued from page ii

W. W. Norton & Company, Inc.: "The Seven Deadly Sins: Anger," from *A Fraction of Darkness* by Linda Pastan. Copyright © 1985 by Linda Pastan. Reprinted by permission of W. W. Norton & Company, Inc.

Academy Chicago Publishers: Excerpt from *A Gathering of Heroes* by Gregory Alan-Williams. Copyright © 1994 by Gregory Alan-Williams. Reprinted by arrangement with Academy Chicago Publishers.